# Cinema

# TALKING IMAGES SERIES

edited by Yann Perreau

**Series ISSN** 1744–9901

forthcoming in the series:

# Cinema
## The Archeology of Film and the Memory of a Century

Jean-Luc Godard & Youssef Ishaghpour

*Translated by John Howe*

*Oxford • New York*

This work is published with the support of the French Ministry of Culture – Centre National du Livre.

This book is supported by the French Ministry for Foreign Affairs, as part of the Burgess programme, headed for the French Embassy in London by the Institut Français du Royaume-Uni.

First published in book form, 2000, by Editions Farrago. © Editions Farrago, 2000, Archéologie du cinéma et mémoire d'une siècle.

English edition
First published in 2005 by
**Berg**
Editorial offices:
First Floor, Angel Court, 81 St Clements Street, Oxford OX4 1AW, UK
175 Fifth Avenue, New York, NY 10010, USA

© Berg 2005

Berg is the imprint of Oxford International Publishers Ltd.

**Library of Congress Cataloging-in-Publication data**
Godard, Jean Luc, 1930-
   [Archéologie du cinema et mémoire d'une siècle. English]
   Cinema : the archeology of film and the memory of a century / Jean-Luc Godard & Youssef Ishaghpour ; translated by John Howe.— English ed.
      p. cm.
   ISBN 1-84520-196-5 (cloth) — ISBN 1-84520-197-3 (pbk.)
1. Motion pictures. I. Ishaghpour, Youssef. II. Title.

   PN1994.G555 2005
   791.43—dc22

                                                                                        2004029767

**British Library Cataloguing-in-Publication data**
A catalogue record for this book is available from the British Library.

ISBN-13  978 1 84520 196 8 (Cloth)
          978 1 84520 197 5

ISBN-10  1 84520 196 5 (Cloth)
          1 84520 197 3 (Paper)

Typeset by JS Typesetting Limited, Porthcawl, Mid Glamorgan
Printed in the United Kingdom by Biddles Ltd, King's Lynn.

**www.bergpublishers.com**

# Contents

**Part II  Jean-Luc Godard, *Cinéaste* of Modern Life: The Poetic in the Historical**

# *Foreword*

We're born in the museum, it's our homeland
after all...

Jean-Luc Godard

The freshness of the Nouvelle Vague (New Wave)
movies that came out of France from 1959 onward
was not simply the product of raw talent, beautiful
monochrome photography and novel jump-cuts
boldly assembled on the hoof. Underlying their narrative approach and often clearly perceptible in their
dialogue is a self-consciously theoretical dimension.
The New Wave was a concrete manifestation of the
distinctive French cinema whose development had
been discussed for over ten years in the columns of
*Les Cahiers du cinéma* and its predecessor *La Revue
du cinéma*. François Truffaut, twenty-eight when *Les
quatre cents coups* was released in 1959, and Jean-
Luc Godard, whose *À bout de souffle* appeared the
following year when he was thirty, had both written
for *Cahiers* from the start.

It is hardly surprising that France, a country where the philosopher Jean-Paul Sartre could enjoy equal billing in the early 1960s with the president Charles de Gaulle and the non-New Wave film star Brigitte Bardot, had been quick to realize that cinema was an art form as well as a vertically integrated cash-generating distribution cartel. Art critics and philosophers took cinema seriously from its first appearance (owed, it should be remembered, more to the inventive Lumières than the businessman Edison); specialist film critics, most of all the great André Bazin, founder of *Cahiers*, established a clipped, precise, informed writing style that few Anglophones can emulate even today; in 1936 Henri Langlois started the collection of old movies at the Cinémathèque française, in whose viewing rooms the New Wave gang spent their teenage years post-World War II. The thriving 1930s cinephile subculture of film societies and reviews resumed with great vigor after the Hollywood-starved occupation years: France in the 1950s was liberally sprinkled with art houses and specialist cinemas showing old and non-mainstream movies, as it still is today.

*À bout de souffle* was Godard's fifth film. Since his first short, *Opération béton* (1954), he has made as director, and often as producer and scriptwriter too, well over a hundred films, more than forty of them full-length features. Some were much admired, some (especially during Godard's Maoist period from 1968 to 1973) attracted harsh criticism; few enjoyed great commercial success. But Godard has continued to make films, quite often films he wanted to make, largely because he is recognized by his peers as a master film maker. Collaborators have always been confident that Godard as a director knew exactly what he was doing. He gained an early reputation for making films exceptionally quickly and cheaply even by New Wave standards.

For a man immersed in cinema since adolescence and an emblematic figure of the French New Wave, Godard is something of a heretic. For a start he is not exactly French, being of Swiss Francophone Protestant and French Huguenot descent. In youth a well-dressed "bourgeois" appearance contrasted with the casual student attire of his fellows; in their often voluble company he was known for his long, withdrawn, thoughtful silences; as a director he has been known to reshoot *at his own expense* sequences that appeared faultless to co-workers. Most of his films have been made in 35 mm, but he has used 16 mm and sometimes both gages. He started to use video as soon as it became available, and much of the recent work, some of it made for television, has mixed video with film.

Even Godard's early films contain explicit references to the physical processes of film making, a reflective and reflexive element that has become central to his work. When Henri Langlois died in 1978 he was scheduled to deliver a series of lectures on the history of cinema at the University of Montreal. Godard was the chosen substitute, and the lectures he gave were published in 1980 as *Introduction à une véritable histoire du cinéma.* A frequent complaint in these lectures was that a verbal discourse alone was inadequate for the purpose: a history of cinema image, Godard thought, should be narrated using that image. Although the lectures had used extracts from Godard's own films and those of other makers as illustrations, he felt that the subordinate role this gave to the image was misleading. This eventually led to the appearance of *Histoire(s) du cinéma,* the main subject of both the texts that follow: four and a half hours of video made for television, widely regarded as Godard's masterpiece.

*Histoire(s) du cinéma* is an extraordinary piece of work, quite unlike anything ever made by anyone else. It can be described broadly as a history of cinema and a history of the twentieth century, each inside the other. A complete work in itself, it is subdivided into four chapters, each with an A and B section, and should be seen simultaneously as one film, four films and eight films. It was composed over a period of twelve or thirteen years, between the mid-1980s and 1998, at the studio in Rolle, Switzerland, where

Godard has lived and worked since the late 1970s. Work was interrupted by other commitments and difficulties with TV production companies, although Godard now says that these delays were beneficial to the final product: a dense collage – I hesitate to use this word, but it will do – of all sorts of film clips, from early film through Hollywood and other cinema to newsreel and video, often processed and overprinted, still photographs and reproductions of paintings, with added captions and subtitles, and snatches of soundtrack similarly pasted over and combined with recorded music of all sorts, broadcast speech, poems and other audio text, the whole assembly cemented together by Godard's own voiceover.

The title itself embodies a sort of diagram of the film's deconstructive/constructive poetic approach. Ostensibly it means: *History of cinema*, with the bracketed "s" suggesting that there may be more than one history of cinema. Like its English equivalent, the word *histoire* also has the related meaning of story or account, but in French common usage it has, when used in the plural, two sarcastic meanings which it does not have in other languages: lies or bullshit, and problems or hassles. And of course there is History with the uppercase: Stalin-Hitler-Henry Ford-Hiroshima history, the real thing. In this work the word *histoire(s)* possesses all these meanings, sometimes one at a time, sometimes all at once.

Godard himself describes the making of *Histoire(s)* as "an act of painting." Although it consists almost entirely of quotations it is neither documentary nor fiction, nor indeed any other recognizable genre of narrative cinema. It is however clearly an ambitious, large-scale and somewhat forbidding work of art, perhaps a great one. Youssef Ishaghpour, the art historian and cinephile whose dialogue with Godard and essay on Godard's genealogy as a modern artist make up this text, compares Godard at different moments to Hegel, Wagner and Rembrandt; Colin McCabe, in his entertaining and informative recent biography of Godard, admits to having called Godard "the great French poet of the twentieth century" (his interlocutor however had "looked at me as if I were an uncultured rustic"). Ishaghpour writes in depth on the poetic in Godard's work, and underlines Godard's insistence on a sort of legal equality between image and text.

I have watched a good deal of *Histoire(s)*[1] and find it hypnotic, imposing and affecting, but so complex and filled with references as to be impossible to follow except in brief, partial flashes. While the *auteur's* voiceover proceeds at a stately pace, with frequent repetitions and long pauses, extremely rapid sequences of retouched and overprinted images fill the screen amid a farrago of music clips and other sound, interspersed with titles and blank screen.

Repeated throughout is the image of 35 mm film whizzing back and forth in time through an editing console, and a rather bullying sound effect of tapping typewriter keys. My emphatic guess would be that even the most learned academic or critical or professional cinephiles would need several or many viewings to come to terms with it as a complete work. Although Godard claims, perhaps not entirely seriously, that the work is easily understood by "sincere people," I do not believe I am alone in finding it difficult, or needing to view sequences repeatedly, look things up and consult cinephile friends.

With the poetic quality of Godard's verbal discourse I am on firmer ground. A few years ago I was given the job of translating into English the transcribed voiceover from *Histoire(s)* for ECM Records of Munich.[2] No text is perfect, of course, but although the work had to be done in a hurry it was not difficult. Translating is not always enjoyable, but this was. Godard's discourse has a crystalline character that makes it drop straight into English and read brilliantly without the need for any crossword-type translator's gymnastics. That limpid quality is present even when, as in the dialogue with Ishaghpour, Godard is speaking off the cuff, with corrections and hesitations: a quality that demands attention even where one disagrees, which makes a dismissive response seem crass or foolhardy.

In the dialogue that follows, originally published in two numbers of the French review *Trafic*, Youssef Ishaghpour persuades and provokes Godard into giving a partial exegesis of *Histoire(s)*, in support of what Colin McCabe calls the "attempt to find an audience on his own terms," something that "might serve as the very definition of modernism." The mechanisms of that modernism and its intellectual and artistic roots are examined in detail in Ishaghpour's scholarly and sympathetic accompanying essay.

John Howe

## Notes

1. About two thirds of it, recorded from TV in the version shown by the Franco-German arts channel, Arte. Apparently there is no available definitive edition of *Histoire(s) du cinéma*. Godard complains that the original videotapes released by Gaumont were of "appalling quality." There is said to be a Japanese DVD edition; DVD seems a good idea for *Histoire(s)* as the technology facilitates rapid leafing back and forth and replaying short sequences.
2. For Jean-Luc Godard, *Histoire(s) du cinéma*, The Complete Soundtrack, ECM New Series, 1999 (4 vols, 5 CDs).

# *Acknowledgments*

Any mistakes or solecisms in the translation are my own, of course, but I am indebted for technical and other information to Chris Darke, Mike Hodges, Laura Mulvey, Geoffrey Nowell-Smith and Yann Perreau.

*John Howe*

# Part I
## Interview

# 1

# *Cinema*

***Youssef Ishaghpour:*** Viewing your *Histoire(s) du cinéma*
one is put in the same situation as you, with your
project, the "plan" you thought unachievable but
achieved nevertheless, as in that Brecht poem. A bit
like St. Augustine starting to write a book and having
a vision of a child trying to move all the water out
of the sea into a small hole with a spoon. We always
come up against the impossibility – the pointlessness
actually – of saying everything, when the real task
is to "say it all." Something that can be done by
creating "a thinking form," like your *Histoire(s)*. But
to "say" those *Histoire(s)* one would have to develop
their Platonic Idea. That would require a breadth of
outlook that is probably hard to achieve without first
establishing a distance from your work, which has no
equivalent either in cinema history or the history of
art in general, or indeed in its approach to History
proper. Only a period of sedimentation would pro-
vide enough distance for this work to be able to

metamorphose into an Idea. But as a spectator, I'm still too close to your *Histoire(s)*. And what sort of history are we talking about, by the way? There's nothing you would expect to find in a textbook: no listing of dates, names and facts in chronological order to describe sequences of events, no methodical cataloging of technologies, schools of thought or great works. You position yourself below the vicissitudes, without avoiding them, and also above them, in a synthetic perspective from which cinema stops being the entertaining spectacle it is generally held to be, or the specialist area it is for cinéphiles, to appear as it really is: not just the major art form of the twentieth century, but the center of the twentieth century, embracing the human totality of that century, from the horror of its disasters to its efforts at redemption through art. So it's about cinema in the century and the century in cinema. This, as you say, is because cinema consists of a particular relationship between reality and fiction. And since its power made cinema the century's manufacturing plant, or in your words made "*the twentieth century exist*," it's as important as any major historical event, and can take its place alongside the others on that basis. But since those events were determined partly by cinema, and were also filmed for cinema newsreels, they're an integral part of cinema; and because, as History, those events acted on the destiny

4

of cinema, they're part of cinema history. "*History of cinema, History of the news, actuality of History*," as you say many times. It's essentially a work of art, not a discourse, so I understand both your wish to talk about what is really a film – and also eight films – and your reluctance to talk about it.

*Jean-Luc Godard*: Well, no, to put it simply I don't have an encyclopedically learned discourse that could be summed up by saying I was trying to do this or I did that. Not at all. It's eight films combined in one, both together. It came like that. But it's eight chapters of a film that could have had hundreds of others, and even more appendices, like the footnotes that are often more interesting to read than the actual text… It's a big book with eight chapters, and that layout didn't budge in ten years. Sort of a dim beacon in the dark to say go this way, "Fatal beauty" at the moment, not "Mastery of the universe"… And the reason why eight, or rather four, with A and B sections: because a house has four walls. Naïve stuff like that.

# 2

# *Constellation and Classification*

*YI*: The transverse and vertical cuts you made to compose this assembly were made initially in reference to an Idea of cinema, based on different aspects of cinema disposed to outline an Idea in the form of a constellation.

*JLG*: Yes, eight constellations, four times two..., the visible and the invisible, and then within that locating, through the traces that exist of them, other constellations..., to cite Benjamin who says that stars, at a given moment, form constellations and there is resonance between the present and the past.

*YI*: On the matter of resonance between past and present, there's an internal relationship with time in your film, even one might say with time upon time, a re-memorizing aspect, resulting partly from the years it took to make.

*JLG*: It certainly did take many years; it took a lot of time. It wasn't planned like that but that's how it was done. And it's none the worse for it, because if I'd had to do it normally all at once, I don't think I would have given it that amount of time. Time has to be endured whatever you do with it.

*YI*: At the beginning of one of the chapters there are two photographs of you, one recent and the other much older, and you pass from one to the other as if we were going back in time. So this re-memorizing isn't only in relation to the century or to the cinema, but also in relation to yourself. In other words there's an autobiographical dimension to the film that is very important, and I believe that, quite apart from your situation in the history of cinema or your attitudes to that history, there's a relationship with time and all that that implies stemming from the length of time needed to make this film. In your *Histoire(s) du cinéma*, perhaps because the passage concerns your relations with cinema history, there's only a single outside element, a single moment that is external to your film, a commentary from outside, and that's your dialogue with Serge Daney.[1]

*JLG*: When *Histoire(s) du cinéma* was first taken up by Gaumont, it had been on hold for three or four years. I hadn't completed my plan, I had only made the first two chapters although there were eight in preparation. At the time Canal+ and a lot of other institutions didn't want to make them. Then Gaumont took the project on, and all of a sudden I found myself wondering how I was going to go about it, where to restart the thing. While making the first two chapters I had taped various things without knowing what to do with them: Alain Cuny reading Élie Faure, Sabine Azéma reciting a text from Broch's *La Mort de Virgile*, Julie Delpy as a schoolgirl reading Baudelaire's *Le Voyage*... I had also spoken about this project, which was still just a project, describing first "All the histories," secondly "A single history," thirdly "Only the cinema," then "Fatal beauty" and others. Daney's article had appeared in *Libération*. But there was a tape of our conversation: I had told him a bit about how I try to work, the difficulties I was having... So I had this tape. When I had to start again, I needed a new point of departure. Each of the parts begins with an introduction. All beginnings have always been very heavy going; it's very difficult because you have to launch yourself and get moving. So I told myself I would start from this recording with Daney. It was television, pretty much, more or less the standard TV interview. But to me Daney was also the end of criticism, as I had known it, which I think started with Diderot:[2] from D to D, Diderot to Daney, only the French make real critics. It's because they're so argumentative. It's also there because what

Daney says sums up quite well what used to be the position of the cinematic Nouvelle Vague...

*YT*: I get the impression though that here too, with the presence of Daney as sole witness, it's not so much a matter of seeking an outside point of view, an objectivization or legitimization, as of trying to integrate the outside world with the inside of your film, in a Hegelian sort of way. Certainly when Daney says to you, on the position of the Nouvelle Vague and your own relations with the history of cinema, "*You alone,*" you answer "*Just cinema.*" What I really think though, and this is why I see you essentially in the tradition of the lyrical poets, is that we're talking about an identity somewhere between "You alone" and "Just cinema," as in your plays on the words "*histoire*" and "*toi,*" although that sends us back to love stories, but as you show in your film love stories are the daily bread of cinema.

*JLG*: It's just me who said just cinema... "*Just cinema.*" I'd said it before, it was in the eight chapters. Daney enabled me to begin, to follow him and then go elsewhere, or when he was talking about something to make a simple illustration, not like showing a photo of Marilyn Monroe when you're talking about her, more like showing a photo of something else to introduce another idea... Not long after the Liberation there was a brief vogue for what were

10

called "*poetic films*," there would be poetry or text and then there was simply illustration. You take a poem or a text and you simply put photos or images on it, then you see either that what you've done is banal, that it's worthless, or that the image you add enters into the text and eventually the text, when the time comes, springs from the images, so there's no longer this simple relationship of illustration, and that makes it possible to exercise your capacity to think and reflect and imagine, to create. That simple form, whether with an interviewer or an illustrated poem, enables you to discover at a stroke things you've never thought of before.

*YI*: From basic raw material that is actually very limited we get an impression of immensity. It's big because it projects. The raw material is limited partly perhaps because you didn't have access to a lot of things, but in another way it seems like a necessity, because no form can be created without what is the elementary basis of form: recurrence, going back, repetition, all differentiated, and it's the work on image, but also on sound, the words, the musics, it's the whole montage that makes that impression possible through the metamorphosis of a limited whole. All the same, handling such a diversity of documents, not only films but newsreels, sound recordings, books, paintings, in a way all the elements of an archive covering the

11

twentieth century, and assembling them in several different ways, must have been pretty gruelling.

*JLG*: I wondered how Cuvier[3] had managed. After you've got things classified you still have to be able to find them again. I had a very simple classification and then a classification with the beginnings of elaboration. The snag then was that I started with some idea of sequences, I'd got a lot of specialized boxes and I could no longer find what I was looking for in the basic box, so then I came back to a simple thing: man, woman, war, child, a very banal system to at least be sure of finding things, and now sometimes I look for them and absolutely can't find them, I know they're there but I don't find them. Which is also a Borges sort of idea: the foundation, the demonstration, is in one of these wrappers, but you don't find it, and even if you do glimpse it in passing you don't recognize it because it isn't as you think it is.

## Notes

1. Serge Daney (1944–92) was an extremely influential cinéphile and film writer who published his first article in *Cahiers du cinéma* at the age of twenty. Editor in chief of *Cahiers* from 1975 to 1981, he subsequently became film and

TV editor of the daily newspaper *Libération* and founded the cinema magazine *Trafic,* which first appeared in 1991. Like Godard and others associated with *Cahiers,* he takes cinema seriously as an art form and views it, and film criticism, in a wider historical and political context.

2. Denis Diderot (1713–84), French philosopher and generalist intellectual, promoter and director of the *Encyclopédie* (first edition 1751), later author of ground-breaking critical writings on the arts (*les Salons*).

3. Georges, baron Cuvier (1769–1832), French zoologist, founder of comparative anatomy and paleontology.

# 3

# Angle and Montage

**YI**: When I read *Introduction à une véritable histoire du cinéma*, the book you had published in the "Ça cinéma" collection, I was very struck by the story of the invention of the angle shot as the precondition for the invention of montage, in Eisenstein especially, but there are so many things in the film that this invention of the angle shot is no longer directly addressed.

**JLG**: When I said "*Just cinema*" I also meant that only in cinema do you find images like that: here's a photo, you only see it in the cinema, you see a train hanging in a ravine, it's not literature, it's Buster Keaton, or a still from Mack Sennett or from Eisenstein, only cinema could have made those images. You only have to look, for example, at some stills from *Pré de Bejine*. There are incredible angles, as only Eisenstein could do them, not at all like Welles's angles, which are a function of thought and so a different thing altogether. In Eisenstein they're formalist angles very like painting or something of the sort. It's easy to see that by putting two angles side by side you get an effect of true montage, which enabled me to say, afterwards, that Eisenstein discovered the angle after Degas and others in painting, and that having discovered the angle he discovered montage...

*YI*: But Degas himself had discovered the angle through photography and because he was a photographer, that's how framing was discovered thanks to photography, then the invention of the angle shot, which was completed by Eisenstein and which he himself defined as the dialectic between the object and the film-maker's judgement...

*JLG*: You put three angle shots of a lion and you have a lion getting up, because of the angles, not because of montage – montage has nothing to say about the lion, it's just a lion – but you have an idea of something getting up, that's where there's a pre-idea of montage. In Nicholas Ray's first film *They Live by Night*, with Cathy O'Donnell, from which I took two or three shots that appear repeatedly in *Histoire(s)*, there's a sequence of four shots of Cathy O'Donnell standing up from a kneeling position, they're not quite centered frontal shots and then they are, and you could say that this is a true beginning of artistic montage. Or as sometimes with Welles (although partly because he would shoot one half of a dialogue in Marrakesh on a Tuesday and the reverse shots a year later in Zurich on a Wednesday), in a simple conversation, there's a sequence of shots like the one in *Arkadin*, where it's more visible, where there's a sort of rhythm that isn't just shot/reverse shot, or from cutting either, but there's a certain rhythm in the dialogue that's just there, that's both a very brilliant effect and something like a trail leading towards what all film makers are after, which is really montage to tell stories in a different way. While there are people who just bandy montage about glibly, for example the girl who does computer stuff on a film by Techiné says she's doing the montage on Techiné's film, but she isn't doing montage any more than the girl who sells you an airline ticket... One could point out that in fact – or in legend anyway, we need legends because they give an image of what has taken place, not necessarily exact – when Griffith invented the closeup because he wanted to approach an actress, the way he did it there was an angle-shot effect, she was shot first frontally and then immediately from a different angle, you could see that in fact there were two different angles, there was no actual approach... In the first chapter of *Histoire(s)*, at one point, there are some things like that that I put in a couple of times, without going into any detail... But this business of angle and montage isn't the whole story... there's a lot of other

17

stuff to be done on cinema. The main work hasn't been done. There were all the appendices. It would have taken a whole crew working on nothing else for five or six years, at least a hundred appendices that I'd like to have made, but that I couldn't manage by myself, anyway without being paid a salary to do it by the CNRS.

# 4

# *The Urgency of the Present/ The Redemption of the Past*

**YI:** In the dialogue with Daney, you say that without cinema you yourself would have had no history, that you were indebted to it for that and you had to repay what you owed it with *Histoire(s)*. That's a personal level essential to the film. But at the end of the sequence you raise a sense of urgency that, while very personal, is of a general order. You talk about cinema not being preserved from time but preserving time (M. Blanchot), you talk about trying in your work to tune your ear to time but also to give it expression, and you contrast that with our time, the totalitarianism of the present, the organization of a unified time whose task is to abolish time (B. Lamarche-Vadel). Isn't it that very disappearance of time, which could be said to be an effect of "real time" information technology and the generalized circulation of image-communications-merchandise through the television screen and its ephemera that destroy the present by obscuring it continuously it as it occurs, isn't it that urgency of the present, the disappearance of time and even the hopelessness it engenders, that also determined the existence of *Histoire(s) du cinéma* as a memoir of the cinema and the century, a memoir of time inside time? Proceeding from the urgency of the present to a salvaging of the past seems to me one of the similarities between your film and what Walter Benjamin hoped to achieve in his book *Paris, capitale du XIXe siècle*. If what has to be saved isn't saved now, Benjamin says, it may vanish for ever, and that's how your film relates to cinema.

*JLG*: Certainly, it felt a bit like that, it's not very clear, it was very unconscious, later on reflection it became more conscious. When you, and many others, quote an author or talk about a book, you've really read it, but with me, I hear a sound, I think it ought to go *here*, there's a mixture...

*YI*: I didn't mean to talk in terms of influence at all, I was looking at the different ways of approaching History and trying to find, by comparison and differentiation, what is specific to your work, for I believe that the object and the approach are different each time. In the film you made with A-M. Miéville on the Museum of Modern Art in New York there are constant references to Benjamin... In him too, in *Paris, capitale du XIXe siècle*, there was this desire to produce a work consisting entirely of archive material and quotes through montage or, as he put it, to build large structures out of small elements chosen and reworked with clarity and precision. Benjamin had been in Moscow, he had seen Vertov's films, and what he wrote about cinema, that it was completely different from the artistic tradition because it was a practice based on the real, was broadly determined by that...

*JLG*: Oh yes... I didn't know that...

# 5

# *History and Re-memorization*

*YI*: This relation between the urgency of the present and the salvaging of the past excludes the sort of history that merely recounts how things have happened, or aspires to explain the past in terms of the present or the present in terms of the past. It demands on the contrary a history that rejects the idea of continuous development and uses a structure that accentuates fissures and jumps to liberate the unrealized forces contained in the past. Then the past assumes its true face, or as you say in one of those oxymoronic inscriptions that start the different parts of your film: "*To give an accurate description of what has never occurred is ... the proper occupation of the historian*" (Oscar Wilde). Since a "true History" cannot be written from the victors' point of view, its purpose being to "wake the dead and save the vanquished," what we find in your film is "re-memorization" rather than history written in the indicative, viewing things from the outside. That was also Péguy's conception in his *Clio* and the reason why he contrasted Michelet[1] with other historians. History is unachievable, because it would take an eternity to compile a history of the shortest time, as Clio says at the end of your film, since for history time is a horizontal line along which there are events. But memory is vertical. History deals with events without ever being inside them. Memory, what Péguy also calls "*aging*," is not always involved with current events but is always inside them, it stays there, running backward and forward through the passing events and sounding their depths. Or to paraphrase Benjamin again, your film isn't the sort of history that deals with wood and ashes, it's the living memory of the flames. There's a history that patrols the cemetery, Péguy says, and another form of history that tries to be "*a resurrection of the past*," a redemption of the past: that's memory, something that can only be realized in a work of art, and your *Histoire(s) du cinéma* is essentially and above all a work of art.

*JLG*: It's cinema, in other words not like literature which is more closely bound to meaning, in film there's rhythm, it's more like music, that's how I came to use black for rhythm...

*YI*: The difference from a historian's work, you spell it out in your film in a JLG/JLG quotation: "*It isn't said, it's written, it's composed, it's painted, it's recorded,"* while a historian's work is essentially spoken. A historian can't allow himself to create "images," as you with montage and collage can bring together unconnected things, because a historian ought to be able to make a rational presentation of all the intermediate relations and mediations. Every time an image appears a mass of connections, interferences and resonances spring up around it. When you raise the Liberation of Paris, there's De Gaulle's speech, there's your image of that epoch, of Resistance people in slow motion, of Duras with the song that mentions Marguerite, and a shot of her book *La Douleur*, there's the commemoration of the Liberation set up for television, and you talk about Debord, but also about Claude Roy who had taken the CNC set up by Vichy... I must be forgetting a lot of things, but if I remember right it ends with a scene from *Pierrot le Fou* concerning some of those same maquisards, who are said to be dead but of whose names and lives we learn nothing. There's always, at every moment, a polyphonic structure, you have up to ten or a dozen levels of different elements, several images and several texts, which don't always go in the same direction. And perhaps that's why it's difficult for historians to accept. Because for them there's a fact and then another, in a relation of cause and effect, while with you it's like a sound in which one can hear not only the harmonics but also the

counterpoints, all in polyphonic simultaneity, and
even the inversions, but also the circular ripples
going out from these things and the links that are
formed at certain moments not directly, but at points
of resonance and intersection between these ripples,
which may be and sometimes are contradictory, as in
music. Crystals out of time, palimpsest, refraction,
echo, flash, this is about memory, about what an
image, like a signal-booster, brings instantly to mind
unleashing a network of further connections. Your
film is a form that thinks and makes people think,
not a discourse in the indicative of a kind associated
with scholarship, perhaps it's a genre not so much
of "Historical philosophy" but of Historical thought,
and the scale of your film places it with musical works,
Wagner, Mahler... Your film is like the century's great
novels, or poetic works intended to be complex and
inclusive, blurring the distinction between prose and
poetry, image and reflection, personal lyricism and
documentary history, and systematically combining
writing and re-memorization to become the place
where the truth of the century resounds. A historian
wouldn't say what you say, referring to Malraux,
about the gaze of Manet's women, but it seems to
me the essence of your film, the gaze through which
the interior encounters the cosmos. Something of
a *Divine Comedy*, exept that each is a unique work,
mining different ore in different times. When we

hear Heidegger's text on poets in times of distress, it's Jean-Luc Godard that we see. I believe the main difference with Braudel for example is the matter of your own place in your film: you are there alongside the other cinéastes and among them. You are also the museum attendant who expects his tip and berates visitors who don't understand that the works are what it's all about. You are the cantor, the orchestral conductor or high priest behind his lectern evoking the old films brought into the present by Langlois.[2] You are also the one who owes his identity and his history to cinema and must repay the debt for his own salvation, and although you say "*History, not its narrator*," you are there as the narrator, not just as the absent fabricator who has placed a card on display. You are also there as one who has been to heaven. One can't help wondering whether Godard, who has found his home in cinema, occupies a place in your *Histoire(s)* equivalent to Hegel's place in his system.

*JLG*: History is stating something at a given moment, and Hegel puts it well when he says you're trying to paint gray on gray. From what little I know of Hegel, what I like about his work is that for me he's a novelist of philosophy, there's a lot of romantic in him...

*YI*: Because he recounts the whole History of the world and the whole history of philosophy, the one inside the other, as a re-memorization and not as chronological history written in the indicative. Incidentally, it's in much the same way, with the aim of totalization, that you recount the history of cinema, and like Hegel you can only do this totalizing because you're present at a final moment in this history of cinema, a sort of closure, when there's nothing left but the repetition and liquidizing of what has been. Although *Histoire(s) du cinéma* comprises multiple histories, juxtaposed and independent of each other, with the connections that arise between them, one nevertheless has the impression of a totalization, apparent in the last part of the film which consists of an entirely subjective history – in any case you say "*All these histories which are my own*" – a subjectivity that is itself the effect of this history.

*JLG*: To me History is, so to speak, the work of works; it contains all of them. History is the family name, there are parents and children, literature, painting, philosophy ... let's say History is the whole lot. So a work of art, if well made, is part of History, if intended as such and if this is artistically apparent. You can get a feeling through it because it is worked artistically. Science doesn't have to do that, and other disciplines haven't done it. It seemed to me that History could be a work of art, something not generally admitted except perhaps by Michelet.

## *Notes*

1. Jules Michelet (1798–1874), French historian noted for humane and lyrical style, author of a nineteen volume history of France and a History of the French Revolution.
2. Henri Langlois (1914–77), co-founded in 1936 (with Georges Franju) the Cinémathèque française, an archive of old films many of which would otherwise have been lost for ever, and remained its director for the rest of his life. Godard, Truffaut, Chabrol and other Nouvelle Vague figures acknowledge their debt to Langlois and the Cinémathèque, Godard explicitly in this text.

# *6*

# *How Video Made the History of Cinema Possible*

*YI*: To return to the image of the interior connecting with the cosmos: in your film there's cinema of course and the century, and at the same time there's art and a reflection on art and image, that's why there's the text on beauty and why you constantly refer to it so that these relations can be established, because there's a dimension of reflection inside the film, of thought becoming form and the resonance of all that in a totality where cinema, life, humanity, art and History are inextricably linked. But for cinema to turn in on itself in this way, in this sort of reflection on itself and its history embracing the entire twentieth century and *its* History – for that to be possible and for the result to become a Scripture, cinema *squared* so to speak, a great work – it seems to me that the existence of video was necessary. Technically first of all, for all the processing of the image, the overprints, captions and so on. But apart from the technical side, isn't video the historical condition making this film possible, since video in a sense also means the end of cinema?

*JLG*: Video seemed to me one of the avatars of cinema, but it's become something rather different in broadcast television where there's no creation at all any more, just broadcasting. But video's going to be overtaken by information technology or some sort of hybrid mixture which will get increasingly remote from cinematic creation as it can still just about exist today. I'd say there was no very big difference between video and cinema and you could use one like the other. There are things you can do better with one so with the other you do something else. Video came from cinema, but you can't say now that IT comes from cinema. The first video cameras and even today, the three colours and things like that, the standard settings are much the same as in cinema, but it's different with what comes from IT theory. *Histoire(s)* was cinema. Technically it was textbook stuff, very simple things. Of the forty possibilities in the list I used one or two, mostly overprinting to help retain the original cinema image, while if I'd tried to do the same thing with film I'd have had to use reverse negative copies and that causes a loss of quality; above all you can alter the image easily with video, while with film all variation has to be preplanned. Incidentally there was no huge console, no team with twenty-five video screens, I didn't even have a video librarian: it was an act of painting. The overprints, all that comes from cinema, they were tricks Méliès used...

*YI*: They were used, but very little...

*JLG*: Because it was more complicated ... besides, I used very few, you get the impression there are a lot, but there are some titles over images, there are a few overprints and that's more or less it...

*YI*: The thing of two images fading into each other...

*JLG*: Which is really the base, it's always two, showing at the start two images rather than one, it's what I call the image, this image made of two, I mean the third image...

*YI*: I still think there's a difference between what cinema did and what you're doing here. When Eisenstein or Vertov put one image and then another, it was really two images that followed one another, each keeping its own meaning, and then, especially with Eisenstein, there was a third image engendered in the spectator's mind, what Eisenstein called creating the image as opposed to representation of a theme...

33

*JLG*: That's all I was doing…

*YI*: But when you use two images in an overprint…

*JLG*: Not all the time, but to remind, to show that it's there…

*YI*: When you talk about what the daily prayer ought to be … saying this daily prayer should be for equality and fraternity between reality and fiction. We see *Les Quatre Cents Coups*, and it's the only emblematic Nouvelle Vague movie in your film. We see Jean-Pierre Léaud running toward the sea on the right, and in overprint there's the end of Fritz Lang's *You Only Live Once*, the couple walking off to the left. What's immediately striking is this double movement in opposite directions, as if there should never be just one direction, and for me that characterizes your whole film. But this contrary movement, along with the resonance produced by this Lang film overlaying the Truffaut film, produces an even more nostalgic character, not just in reference to the death of Truffaut who was your friend or death in general and time which is one of the themes of the film, but also as the beginning of an idea of the end of the art's childhood and a new birth. An impression confirmed later on when you talk about the illusions of the Nouvelle Vague, behaving as if Stroheim hadn't been destroyed or Vigo dragged through the mud, and show a location photo of Truffaut and Léaud while quoting a text, by Brecht I think, saying that if courage had been beaten it was through weakness.

*JLG*: But those two shots could have been shown separately... I was just saying it's cinema, but I didn't mean cinema in the theoretical discourse sense...

*YI*: Your film isn't a theoretical discourse, it's cinema to the power of two... The way you use overprinting, I mean your two images to create the third, that immediately becomes a mental image, but a remembered image. In the sequence "Cinéma, redisonsle" ("Let's restate cinema") there's the moment devoted to escapist cinema, and you've used on what I think is a shot of Bergman, the image of a woman in long shot outside an open door with a bicycle in the foreground, in other words on what is already an image of the wish to leave, two overprints from *Marnie*, the first with Tippi Hedren moving from right to left with a bunch of white flowers, which dissolves when she is near the middle of the screen, and in the second she's on the left picking up a vase of red gladioli and moving to the right, again disappearing in the centre of the image: these are instantly remembered images...

*JLG*: Yes, from that angle I'd say that *Histoire(s) du cinéma* is the product of thirty years of video, because

I was interested in it from the very beginning, but cinema people weren't, even Sony wasn't interested... When *La Chinoise* was being made, I'd seen a camera and video recorder in Philips's window, and said to myself that the discussion in the room between the Maoists could be filmed on video by them and they could then make their autocritiques, as the fashion then was. We went to see Philips, it was a bit like getting into the defense ministry at the time ... remember it was thirty years ago. But video is, in real-estate parlance, an adjacent wing of cinema. It's paracinema that can be used, in a way, to do what cinema couldn't do without loss of quality – that's it really – and more cheaply too...

*YI*: But there's something else too, video has archived cinema...

*JLG*: It's a child, a natural daughter of cinema...

*YI*: A natural daughter that, the way you use it, embraced the whole of cinema and enabled you to achieve a sort of totalization.

*JLG*: That actually made it possible to narrate it because it wasn't technically possible on film... At one time I'd tried things in *cinémathèques*, with clips of film, five minutes of one, then another and so on, loading films on two projectors. That produced amazing things; you really got the feeling of time and that for me is what History is... You seldom get this feeling with historians, just with Koyré[1] and the transformation of the world image and with Canguilhem[2] of course...

*YI*: I'd like to go back to my idea of video making it possible to store the whole of cinema in reusable archives. I believe that in the cinema image there was still, because of the print, the trace, a magical element, and that the way you use video in relation to cinema approximates to Malraux's position. Works of art, which as works had possessed a sacred meaning, lost that meaning because photography, which archived all works and enabled all sorts of connections to be made between images, had put them in the *Musée imaginaire*.[3] The ability to archive cinema with video resembles the ability to archive works of art with photography...

*JLG*: Absolutely, but Malraux was strictly, broadly a novelist, or writer, and without photography he wouldn't have done the *Musée imaginaire*. But later on, when you read the later books, you feel he knows a phenomenal amount and strangely, the photos again become illustrations of the text. There are extraordinary things, for example his description of how painters at a certain moment painted eternal woman as against the Virgin Mary, that's an image, but the image is more in the text than the photo...

37

*YI*: It's because the last texts, *L'Irréel* or *L'Intemporel,* are essentially chronological texts and no longer synthetic, without all the connections made possible by photography in the earlier texts...

*JLG*: The very earliest ones, with a term that's no longer used: *psychology of art.*

*YI*: While you were making *Histoire(s)* in video, you went on making cinema, as you say straightforwardly, with one image following another, then you recently made with A.-M. Miéville, in video, a film about MOMA and art at the end of the twentieth century, *The Old Place*...

*JLG*: I always thought video was for making "studies." But in practical, financial terms we can't keep going any longer. Or we'd have to start a small business and live partly on advertising, which could subsidize some of our own stuff. But actually in cinema one thing quickly bleeds into another, which is why I've never really believed in that, I've never believed in novelists writing pulp fiction to earn money and then doing their serious novels. That doesn't happen, fortunately... There's another way of working, if you like, with CD-ROM, which gives the added possibility of leafing quickly back and forth, finding things, sticking titles in ... it's like a corridor lined with open doors, a lot of games work like that... Somewhere between the video game and the CD-ROM there could be another way of making films, which would be a lot closer to Borges and people like him. But it'll never be done, we needn't worry... Perhaps one day there will be someone, a Chris or a Van der Keuken, who will make that sort of film... I find though that Van der Keuken for example doesn't dominate the stuff at all, it's either very cinema or too video-arcade and you lose the thread, it needs a comprehensive key. In my case, with *Histoire(s)*, no key is needed.

## Notes

1. Alexandre Koyré (1882–1964), French philosopher of Russian origin, wrote on history and philosophy of science.
2. Georges Canguilhem (1904–95), French philosopher. Succeeded Gaston Bachelard as Director of History and Science Institute at the Sorbonne 1955–71, where he taught Michel Foucault among others. Major theoretician and philosopher of science. Wrote a critical history of concept formation (1955).
3. André Malraux (1901–76), French novelist, writer and politician. *Le Musée imaginaire* (1947) was the first of several works on the history and philosophy of art.

# 7

# *Only Cinema Can Narrate its Own History: Quotation and Montage*

**YI**: Although it uses video your film is cinema, and I think only cinema could narrate its own history while being and remaining cinema to the power of two: painting or music, even literature, can't do it. Because cinema is first and foremost a means of recording and reproduction and because it includes the relation between the two different elements of image and sound. It's because of that that you can make your film by weaving the whole history of cinema out of quotations from films, something no other art can do. The work on itself that cinema makes possible through video enables you to give the quotation as such, and at the same time rework it and appropriate it as an element in your film. The simultaneous functioning made possible by cinema would be impossible even in literature; it couldn't manage that sort of polyphony without risking cacophony.

*JLG*: Absolutely... A history of literature made from existing text would stop being a book immediately and become unreadable. You wouldn't have much idea what it was talking about. It couldn't have three words from Dante and then a bit of Proust while developing its own thinking at the same time...

*YI*: The quotation is taken out of its context, prised out of the continuity of which it was part, and thus acquires a meaning that's stronger and at the same time different, because a resonance takes place with other quotations to create an image, a spark struck from the impact between discontinuous and heterogeneous elements that, on one level, of what might be called collage, retain their heterogeneity and independence, while entering into relation with the other elements through montage. But the quotations are reworked by you, even in the case of extracts from a single film. I give as an example *Duel in the Sun*, where you're saying that cinema showed, but as uncertainty wasn't wanted tales of sex and death were told...

*JLG*: That's a beautiful image, something from the nineteenth century that I got out of a very fine book by François Jacob, *La Logique du vivant*.

*YI*: The quotes aren't only from films and recorded archives, there are some from major texts which you also manage to make into images. For the way you deal with quotes, let me return to my example of *Duel in the Sun*, when the mortally wounded Jennifer Jones climbs, rifle in hand, towards the dying Gregory Peck, whom she has shot. Firstly there's the scene itself being quoted. But at the same time this scene becomes emblematic of the entire film: the part standing for the whole, its metaphor. And it also becomes a metaphor for the whole of cinema through your statement that cinema is stories of sex and death. But at the same time you've re-edited the scene by incorporating two different musics: one the theme music, so to speak, for the mythic cinema of sex and death, the other a nostalgic song about time and a girl, and this music sets up a resonance with the desperate effort being made by Jennifer Jones, whose hand is shown weakening, to arrive in time. On top of that, there's the caption of one of the central ideas of your film, "*the image will come at the time of resurrection,*" with the "*au*" changed to make it read: "*the image will come oh time of resurrection*" to express a longing for that time, with a hint of hope nevertheless of something beyond the present death. So there's the quotation, the power of the thing itself, and at the same time its incorporation into your film. I think your *Histoire(s) du cinéma* has a

43

role of destruction in relation to mythic cinema and also of redemption, of "resurrection." And it can be seen very clearly in this example, because in another chapter, when you talk about love being the ultimate fulfillment of the spirit, once again there's the image of the last kiss between Jennifer Jones and Gregory Peck. And on this repeat there's an overprint of armed forces and the text is talking about the State, while in the last chapter you quote Bataille to show the opposition between the State and lovers. That's why there's cinema to the power of two in your *Histoire(s) du cinéma*, because every time, whether it's with an image from *Faust* or one of Cyd Charisse, or indeed with any other quotation, you superimpose and bring together cinematic opposites, the force of the original film you're quoting and at the same time something carried across from the mythic dimension to an artistic one of your own. At every moment the whole of cinema is present, and at the same time it's present because you're doing something else with it.

# 8

# Histoire(s) du cinéma: *Films and Books*

**JLG**: At the same time what ought perhaps also to have been done ... one of the appendices might have taken a text by Mitry[1] or Sadoul,[2] then made a first power, then a second power, a third, a fourth, and then come back to a first power that covers all the others. That's what we ought to have been able to do, but for that there would have had to be several people thinking together, the way scientists work and their great strength. It ought to be possible in cinema. It was possible, because cinema is made by groups of individuals working together, and then there were always meetings and discussions, even if they only happened in the studio canteen. It used to be possible, but then the notion of the *auteur* arrived bringing solitude. Becker didn't feel alone at all, unlike Straub or me. These stories ought to have been told historically, in any case by cinema historians. At the time of Jean-Georges Auriol's *La Revue du cinéma*

they used to have discussions with each other and then that raised the possibility of a French cinema as distinct from the others. They used to talk to each other although they felt separate.

*YI*: These days there's no discussion between philosophers, painters or writers...

*JLG*: It's because of television and computers. It's the triumph of Edison, because Edison wanted cinema for one person at a time while Lumière... All those philosophers, it's a pity they didn't make cinema... Deleuze[3] was tempted, but instead of making a film he wrote "a book about"...

*YI*: Oh come on, that's not how films are made. Deleuze could never have made films. You don't cobble yourself up into a philosopher or film maker just like that, it takes years and years of work and gifts as well.

*JLG*: But he could have collaborated...

*YI*: But the result of such a collaboration would have been appalling! There's no shortage of examples...

*JLG*: People who did collaborate, like Sollers with Fargier and more recently with Labarthe, the result's really nowhere. The text is so dominant, the intention of the text, the intention to legislate ... but when Sollers writes his literary criticisms it's far better, he makes images. I made a whole film out of that: he had written once that if you want to do theatre in Sarajevo you should play Marivaux and not Beckett, that's a film, that's a moment in a film, whether it's written or filmed makes no difference. But Deleuze's books on film are weaker than his philosophical writings.

*YI*: In his case it was the matter of an external object. Deleuze didn't claim to produce images but concepts, with their own function and purpose. For a philosopher truth, if we can still use the word, is of the order of concepts. That's why philosophers ever since Plato have been generally hostile to images. For you, though, truth is essentially, indeed I'd say exclusively, of the order of images, both in the material sense of an image and in the metaphorical sense of the third image generated by juxtapositions. Deleuze tried to develop a body of thought on image. With you it's the opposite, more the creation of image thoughts. The book of cinema was to be a film made by a film maker. In your case, it took fifty years of cinema to make those *Histoire(s)*.

*JLG*: But the four books of mine published by Gallimard are books of cinema... Earlier on I wasn't really looking, but unconsciously that's where I've always been. It started quite quickly, when I'd done a special issue of *Cahiers*, it was No. 300, in which there was already this way of working with a photo

47

and a text that didn't exist separately... Benjamin says that in the beginning is understanding, in other words hearing as much as seeing, and to say one understands is to say two things, yes I hear what you say and yes I apprehend what you say. In my opinion these are two different things that go together and are indissociable. So you can say crudely that there is image and text. In my view they were on a socially equal footing from the start; one may come first at a given moment and the other second, one can be stronger than the other for a moment, but without any inequality at the start or finish... It was here, if you like, that the whole thing was badly misunderstood, and misunderstood by the distributor Gaumont, which brought *Histoire(s)* out like this... I wanted to do it in the usual way: television showing, books after that, perhaps high-quality videocassettes later. They did the opposite: books first, then cassettes – of appalling quality – with television still to come who knows when. I wanted to put on a small exhibition or something of that sort in a gallery, assemble something that would show the different modes of entering and leaving what one can call History. Because for me the book is what will remain afterwards, books survive longer. Apart from that it has a small audience, a small print run of a book isn't felt to be shaming, but in cinema it is and actually it's very rare. There are secondhand

bookshops but there's no secondhand cinema ...
there are people who collect rare films and there are
archivists, but that's different from books published
in small numbers that you can still track down in
bookshops. In cinema if you search for something
it's as a collector, it's something rare or hard to get
hold of. There's no escaping this difference from
books. I've noticed how *cinémathèque* managers see
it... There's no respect for the videocassette, but
there is respect for the book as a book, that's why
I insisted on it. But also because sometimes, in the
book, you perceive much more clearly if you want
to (I know that generally one doesn't want to), you
perceive much more clearly the equivalence or
fraternity or equality between the photo and the
text, which are on strictly equal footing, things that
completely disorient historians but don't disorient
film people. But they don't want that, people who
talk about films; they want illustration and their
separate text, in which they can exercise a certain
learning and a certain power. They do texts, and
that's the snag. Rather than taking three images
simply and arranging them differently, going too far
and remaking cinema. They could be doing that,
but they aren't, they want to do text... The book has
more of that than the film proper, the book shows
this relation between image and text. They may say
the book hasn't got everything the film has, it hasn't

got all the sound, it hasn't got all the tricks ... no
matter, more of it comes through, while with the film
audience, except for sincere people, it gets lost.

*YI*: It comes through in the book because it's material-
ized, objectivized, while with the film, unless you
constantly freeze the projection, there's a complex
polyphony coming at you at every moment without
all the connections being immediately decipherable,
because it runs in time, it's a form of time, the book
is a form of space.

*JLG*: I'd say there were both; that where there's a
space, where real work is done, is between the text
and the image. I paid homage to image and sound,
my duty or filial respects as it were, to the images
and sounds that came before me. But I also paid
the same homage, the same respects and duty, to
books and literature, and to criticism as I understand
it. And I would have liked literary critics or people
concerned with art and books on art to talk about
it... I'd say that in films there's the spectacle of
History, living History almost, really that's what
cinema does, it's a living image of the unfolding of
History and the tempo of History. And in the book,
which seems like a copy, just an abridged copy,
in fact there's something better still, the memory
of History, because it's written and printed in the
book tradition. To make use of the way the media
of that time serenaded us about existentialism when

I was at school... I didn't know much about it but I remember the phrase: *"For existentialism, existence precedes essence, while before it essence preceded existence."* There you were, you understood something, you felt something, and so you had an image... I'd say books are essence, films are existence, yes, to make use of those images I can put it like that. Since the book came out first, I thought the book would now be a sort of preface, that what had originally been an afterword would assume the function of a preface, a kind of trailer, an "announcement to cinema," a heraldic flourish... But when you read the book without seeing, it's relatively incomprehensible. It's like a maths textbook, you say I don't see, because people nowadays don't know how to see a photo and a text without trying to interpret them... There has to be a key, either comprehensive or explanatory. You have to know whether it's tennis or rugby; if it's just two players knocking a ball back and forth it's meaningless, you're far less capable of appreciating or not appreciating...

*YI*: I think that's the effect of television which constantly designates. Nothing is ever shown unless it is claimed to have been defined already, and this is the affirmation you see where there's no longer anything to see: neither reality nor image, as you say, when you're talking on the box. On television, you assign names to hapless objects.

*JLG*: A book will be left that talks about cinema in a different way from Sadoul and Mitry. One isn't forced to make phrases about that...

*YI*: One isn't forced to make phrases. You constantly say: "a form that thinks."

*JLG*: Quite. A form that thinks. Absolutely...

## Notes

1. Jean Mitry (1907–88), film theorist, critic and film-maker, co-founder of France's first film society and later of the Cinémathèque. His *Esthétique et psychologie du cinéma* (1963) is regarded as a seminal scholarly work on film. Used his own short films to illustrate lectures.
2. Georges Sadoul (1904–67), French Marxist film critic, historian and theorist. Writings include a general history of cinema in six volumes and a biography of Charlie Chaplin.
3. Gilles Deleuze (1925–95), French philosopher. With Michel Foucault, rejuvenated teaching of philosophy in French universities during the 1970s; in collaboration with Felix Guattari wrote *L'Anti-Oedipe*, a critical reassessment of psychoanalysis. Wrote extensively on painting and cinema.

# 9

# *History and Archeology*

**YI**: Your book and your film are very different from the work of these historians. And even given that there are different ways of writing History, your film should really be considered more as an archeology of cinema, archeology in Foucault's sense, not in the usual sense of an archeology that examines traces from the past to establish the factual genesis of things, but one that uses different moments and monuments as the basis for constructs that may seem questionable. It deals with essential relations even though these are not found purely in the world of anterior facts, like a sequence of events. As we shall see, independently of what we can call the internal archeology of cinema or the archeological relation between the history of cinema and History, thus the place of cinema in the twentieth century, there are also the underlying mental conditions or conditions of sensibility, where hidden relations are present; so it reaches all the origins of cinema, all the births of cinema, origin here meaning primal furnace as the origin of something and also what is fundamental to something. For example, when you link the American shot to man, revolver and male genitals, the chest shot to woman and the nurses who figure in all love stories, or (citing Pagnol) the closeup to the royal portrait on coins and that in turn to a Velasquez painting and an image of Bessie Love, you are able to connect the three constituent elements of the star image: closeup, money and charisma. Or with Freud, Charcot and the hysteric who "shows" followed by the image of Lilian Gish on her ice floe, also "showing." That too is the archeology of cinema, even if no one can demonstrate it...

*JLG*: It's what we called, in *The Old Place*, simple juxtapositions that make it possible to tell a story. If you just go forward with one text you miss it, however talented you are, while if you put two texts or two photos together... It's like the story of the stateless people, they conflated two texts and were told they had no right to use one for the other, but they answered: "*In 1940 there was one word and now there's another, virtually the same word, it doesn't mean anything different.*"

*YI*: Your juxtaposition of the story of the prisoner with that of the projection of geometric figures and cinema is archeology too...

*JLG*: Oddly enough there are critics who accuse me of inventing that, but I got it from a book on the history of mathematics. It may be invented but I don't think so... Jean-Victor Poncelet was an engineer officer imprisoned in Russia, and the rest's easy to imagine. All prisoners, except those being tortured, "escape" by thinking. To survive they do gymnastic exercises, and intellectuals work out in their heads the theories they will write when they come out of prison, it's a little story that might have come from Canguilhem or Koyré.

*YI*: It immediately takes on another dimension because Baudelaire comes next and his poem is directly concerned with boredom, with prison and the desire to leave: another archeology of cinema on the level of imagination or sensibility. Baudelaire wrote that poem at a time when boredom was establishing itself historically as a chronic factor in a disenchanted world, combining it with the idea of prison and thus the longing to depart and to travel, which you associate with the childhood of art. In other words the desire to make cinema – since there were film-makers about at the time – but at the same time there's the discovery that it's the same unending sin, the same horror in the same desert of ennui, and thus the same repetition and the same kind of fall.

*JLG*: Having that poem read gave me a lot of thoughts, that others perhaps had had already but that came to me suddenly. I understood that Baudelaire, in fact, did not write that poem at that time by chance, and that it described cinema... Even finally on the level of the text ... at one point it says "*run across our minds stretched like canvases, your memories in the horizon's frame,*" that's certainly a cinema screen as well, he'd never seen one but he foresaw it, as it were. That's why I made someone recite the poem to Michel Piccoli, when I made *2 X 50 ans de cinéma français* with A.-M. Miéville, with Piccoli, who is running the commemoration, realizing all at once that Baudelaire was really foretelling cinema. Or that Charles Cros foretold it, that a poem by Charles Cros – I bought his book because I used to verify my imaginative sources – a poem by Cros called *Le collier des griffes* (Necklace of Claws) was foretelling cinema. Charles Cros is not just anyone in connection with cinema, he invented or theorized things for cinema, he was one of the inventors of cinema at that time, and later, to move film through the gate, the device was called the claw, it could have been called the tooth but the word used was claw, so *Le collier des griffes* corresponded to – predicted – perforated film.

*YI*: After Baudelaire there's Proust, with the idea of lost time and recovered time. With Proust in fact the idea of time is very clearly the idea of memory as against photography, which is the trace of death, of disappearance – you say repeatedly in the film that photography was invented with the colours of mourning, black and white – while memory is recovered time. That's what you do with *Histoire(s)*: you feel cinema ought to have been this refuge for time. And in that connection there are several quotes from *The Magnificent Ambersons*, the ball scene first, and Major Amberson meditating over the fire, which you show for the first time just before the Broch text on beauty, memory and going back, and a second time, before some images from *Arkadin* and while you're referring to Proust. *The Magnificent Ambersons* is not only a film about time. Through these images it associates itself with photographs from the period, and Welles was trying to make a generic product with photographs. It's a film on technique, the one that invented photography and destroys time, but that same technique, cinema, has become a means of salvaging time. The same determination by photography is present in Manet, whose painting can be defined essentially as reduction to what is seen. Which manifests itself in the call of the gaze, of his images of women looking out at the viewer, and you could say that the mediation of the mirror in *Un bar aux Folies-Bergère* was a first sketch of shot/reverse shot. Women who are also looking elsewhere, answering the call of the outside, with a gaze (you say citing Malraux) that joins the interior to the cosmos: for you yet another archeological moment, the birth of modern painting, in other words cinema, in other words an art that thinks, which might be considered the best definition of your own *Histoire(s) du cinéma.*

# 10

# *The History of Love, of the Eye, and of the Gaze*

**YI**: *Histoire(s)* with an *s* is obviously plural history, but doesn't that *s*, in French, introduce the idea of fable, of story … the very thing historians have been trying to dissociate themselves from since Thucydides?

**JLG**: It was to play on the different meanings, the way *histoires* can mean tall stories or hassles. It was to point out that it's both History with a big H and *histoires* with a small one, French has these different usages for the word but other languages don't.

**YI**: From the start, with James Stewart and his tele-photo lens in *Rear Window* or with Mischa Auer, the performing flea trainer in *Arkadin*, and his enormous eye behind its jeweller's glass, and similarly at the beginning of most chapters with the camera and projector, cinema appears as a story of eye and gaze. To that is linked the desire to look associated with

59

pornography and also the romance and love, which are not just in the films but also in the spectator's relation to the films. For example, at the beginning of the first chapter, the character with his back to the camera watching a kiss taken from *Pierrot le Fou*. Or in other places yourself, not only in front of the image of Ava Gardner in *Pandora* but also the image of Robert Mitchum and a woman, with your mouth open almost as if to swallow them. Or again, right at the end of the last film, after a flashback to Mischa Auer and his enormous glass, and as counterpoint and return to the theme of fidelity stated at the beginning of this last chapter, the "scene" from *Othello* – I say "scene" because you've re-edited this Welles film as you have others – a film on the dual gaze, the amorous and possessive gaze and the envious gaze, since you end the scene with the image of Iago, who has been spying on Desdemona, behind her in the deep background. At several other places in *Histoire(s)* you've put shots of Desdemona's strangulation, of her dying face under the sheet that covers it like a shroud or a screen, in what is essentially a film about the gaze, love and image. Or again in Broch's text on beauty, there's the idea of time, of desire, of memory, that finds a resonance with the song at the beginning of the same chapter ... the letter from Paul Valéry talking to a woman about memory and love, while what one sees is a series of portraits of woman writers. Or these women's gazes in closeup, in the last chapter, when the invisible mass of the universe is being discussed – gazes that seem to echo what you say earlier about Manet's women whose gaze connects the interior and the cosmos. Love being, in *Histoire(s)*, the invisible other of pornography, the non-material part, the ultimate fulfillment of the spirit that redeems cinema from being merely a matter of sex and death. Thus I believe that here, too, you differ from a historian, who might mention romance or the desire to see in cinema, who might say that basically cinema only tells "*love stories about girls and boys*" – things a lot of people have said – but who couldn't live this history of cinema as a love story, as you do in your film and in your biography.

*JLG*: They couldn't really. Michelet didn't do it, but he could have. He might have.

# *11*

# *Hitchcock and the Power of Cinema*

*YI*: You start your film with the image of James Stewart and his camera, as it were the quintessential cinematic man, and in the seventh chapter, "Control of the universe," you say of Hitchcock that he's the greatest creator of form of the twentieth century ... poetic licence perhaps...

*JLG*: Er ... it was Hitchcock who said: when you say something, say it twice...

*YI*: But Hitchcock in a way is the opposite of what you do in your films. Do you think that's what cinema ought to have been and wasn't, or is it the other way round? Because elsewhere you use Hitchcock and *Marnie* as the exemplar of the death industry, the cosmetics industry, the lies industry, the escapism industry. Or is that cinema the cinema of fiction and opera as opposed to reality? Is that the magical and fictional power of cinema? What is it that distinguishes Hitchcock from the rest, for you?

*JLG*: Big or small, I haven't thought about the differences, they're equal ... there aren't any small masters, they're all in the big book ... Hitchcock is emblematic of a particular moment, he achieved success by doing difficult things, which is rare. I wouldn't call *Rio Bravo* a difficult film, but *Psycho* isn't an easy film at all. It's a very strange film; there's a whole hour at the beginning in which nothing happens. Hitchcock did difficult things and was enormously successful. Still is today. It wasn't to say that's what the cinema ought to have been, it's just a chapter, like the one on Howard Hughes...

*YI*: It's a bit more than that, he has a place equal to Italian cinema or the Nouvelle Vague. Hitchcock had success with difficult films because he's classical in the true sense. In other words his works can be appreciated just as they are and understood on very different levels, simple or complex, depending on the spectator.

*JLG*: He was fairly universal, he made people shiver everywhere. And he made thrillers that are also equivalent to works of literature... When I say he had control of the universe, the point is that he acquired that control without financial or other violence, while others, producers, and not only producers, wanted it but didn't get it despite all their violence, while he did it simply with images... This chapter could perhaps have been done with someone else, but there was a period when Hitchcock made seven or eight films in succession that are perfect, that were emblematic, because they extended cinema itself, because they were based on the philosophy of cinema...

*YI*: Yes, there's almost a sort of pre-established harmony between Hitchcock and cinema. Benjamin pointed out that photography, modern criminology and the "detective novel" belong to a single constellation, one in which absolutely any random fact or object works as a pointer and anyone at all may be a criminal. The only "adventure stories" in modern society are different kinds of "thriller" in which the extraordinary never strays outside everyday life, but even the most ordinary things start becoming signs, and any sign may lead to another, with the desire to see and know that's inherent in photography, what Benjamin called the psychoanalysis of vision. This metamorphosis of random objects into signs is one of the foundations of cinema. The other is montage, and here you repeat the words of Hitchcock who elsewhere often refers to Koulechev's so-called experiment on the link between two images, formed by the logic of fantasy and involving the spectator's imagination and desires in the film. It's on this double particularity of cinema that the strength of Hitchcock's films is based, putting to work those powers of cinema: image, fiction, fantasy logic and affect. On one level the spectator projects into it his fears and desires, the hopes being realized bringing about their punishment with nightmare implacability; on this level most of his films work like models of myth, and owe their success to that. Hitchcock understood what might be called the underlying power of cinema and put it to work. But on a second level there's something that isn't necessarily obvious to everyone: the matter of making the dreamer aware of his dream and the way all that works and arises, through a sort of irony sometimes or internal self-reflexivity.

*JLG*: That's why Hitchcock seems to me emblematic of cinema.

# 12

# The Loss of the Magic of Cinema and the Nouvelle Vague

**YI:** That sort of fervent admiration nevertheless accompanied by reservations: I sometimes get the impression it's your attitude, if not to cinema in general, certainly to a lot of films. But as with the oxymorons you affect at the start of the chapters, there's often a coexistence of opposites with you: at the very moment you're dealing with escapist cinema, you splice in a small sequence accompanied by the soundtrack from *Johnny Guitar*, which is extremely moving. Your film has a sort of love-hate for Hollywood – a feeling others share – both fascination and repulsion. You call on Rapahaël's Archangel to destroy the Hydra of Babylon, but the image of John Wayne and Natalie Wood in *The Searchers* recurs constantly in your film like an obsession. It's an attitude of destruction and salvage, as if there might have been despite everything a promise in the "dream factory" that ought not to be lost.

*JLG*: The entire planet is willing, as I still am myself sometimes on a Saturday, to go and watch an American film with an ice-cream cone, rather than going just from time to time to see a proper film.

*YI*: Because it was made with a view to leisure-time entertainment, Hollywood people never denied it: they proclaimed it as their sole aim. They never claimed to be producing art, it was you and your *Cahiers* friends who transformed Hollywood into great art.

*JLG*: There's never been art history in America, art quickly became connected with money, and the few artists who weren't were very lonely, even the writers, the ones who tried like Chandler and Hemingway ended by committing suicide in one way or another... But it's a real mystery: why do people like a bad American film and prefer it to, say, a bad Norwegian film?

*YI*: Perhaps because one is "Cinema" and the other less so...

*JLG*: Not these days...

*YI*: Of course. What had a destructive effect on cinema was the generalization of television and the relations of communication established by it. The result's been passge from a world of magic, illusion and fiction to a world of fake and simulacrum, where it's thought sufficient to show all the available money on screen and hope that will yield something. It's the difference between a Thalberg or Hughes and a Spielberg... You were talking about solitude being a recent feeling in cinema where people usually worked together. I believe that from a certain moment cinema was divided, in the same way as literature and painting in the nineteenth century: Flaubert had to separate himself from the serial writers, but not Balzac or Hugo; Courbet and Manet had to stand up against the grandiose painting that predominated in their time. In fact American cinema wasn't dead until *Rio Bravo* and *Touch of Evil*, both incidentally given privileged places in your film. That was the moment when the television-communications circuit became preponderant, causing the same loss of aura to cinema that photography did to painting or the mass-circulation press to literature in the nineteenth century. That was what put an end to that sort of cinema, and that was just when you appeared, you the Nouvelle Vague but most of all you Jean-Luc Godard, because although now you go back to the Second World War, at the beginning your cinema was made, not perhaps entirely consciously, in relation to the new world of image and communication and media that was being established. If cinema can be termed a hot medium, there's something cold, something frigid about television, and that's what produced deepfrozen cinema, if I can call it that; while you no longer wanted or were no longer able to continue with the old cinema. You could take things from Hollywood cinema but you could no longer extend it, at that moment it was all over, but you could carry on by turning it over and and examining it intellectually...

*JLG*: We're born in the museum, it's our homeland after all, we're the only ones...

*YI*: You've given almost a whole chapter to that, and Langlois in front of the engraving of one of the first projections of a moving image appears often in your *Histoire(s)*, but in this particular chapter you replace the engraving with the angel and Virgin from an Annunciation by Botticelli, thus recalling your metaphor of "*cinema like Christianity.*" Langlois didn't reveal cinema but he "confirmed" it for you, you say; he gave you the past you lacked, "*a past metamorphosed into the present.*" It's also the most self-referential chapter: to yourself, your images, your *Alphaville* in overprint or alternation with *Les Trois Lumières*, it's the chapter in which cinema, with nothing from outside, refers to itself, to its own history and not to History. But I'm not so sure that the Nouvelle Vague was alone in its relation to the museum, it seems to me there was a bit of that in Welles...

*JLG*: But he existed before arriving in cinema, in radio and the theatre ... while we were born in the museum, we didn't exist before that. Before that we were readers of reviews and these reviews led us to the museum...

*YI*: But I meant in relation to cinema. Because compared to the founding fathers, Welles was a latecomer. When Welles arrived in Hollywood, to everyone's astonishment, he wanted most to see old films, and in New York he used to have old European films shown... Welles went looking for the museum, *Citizen Kane*'s a film about the history of cinema and the museum...

*JLG*: In a way, yes, he did need the museum, absolutely...

*YI*: I believe there's a place for Welles in relation to the Nouvelle Vague that's been obscured because of Rossellini, and besides, your chapter on the Nouvelle Vague immediately follows the one on neorealism. I think Welles is the other figure, anyway in your particular case especially; I think your early films are a lot closer to *Lady from Shanghai* than to anything by Rossellini.

71

*JLG*: That's true, very much so, *Le Petit Soldat* came out of *Lady from Shanghai*. Perhaps Rossellini was favored because Welles was God to Bazin,[1] thus the parental God, and we needed to differentiate ourselves from our parents.

## Note

1. André Bazin (1918–58), French critic and theorist. Founded a cinema club that showed banned films during the Nazi occupation. Started (1947) *La Revue du cinéma* and in 1951 co-founded, with Jacques Doniol-Valcroze, *Les Cahiers du cinéma*. Saw documentary as "purest" form of cinema, but later partly responsible for formulation of the "auteur theory" associated with the Nouvelle Vague. Seen as father of modern film criticism.

# 13

# *Before and After Auschwitz*

*YI*: When you say that with Manet begins modern painting, that is, cinema, in other words an art making its way towards the word, towards, in fact, forms that think, you add that the flame finally went out at Auschwitz...

*JLG*: It's a bit sudden, but yes, the possibility of thinking was extinguished at that moment.

*YI*: You believe there was really thought in cinema before that?

*JLG*: Even if it wasn't entirely successful, there was the hope. Similarly, when you read Resistance histories, after '42 or '43 even the people in Algiers, the simpler ones who had nothing to do with politics and didn't want to, were saying: *"We've worked and it's been for nothing, you can see how it's going to be, it's going to be the same as before."* The opportunity wasn't seized. As for the emblematic element, that wasn't me, it was the camps... And it took me quite a while to understand it, because no one taught me about it at the time...

*YI*: I didn't mean it like that at all, I agree with you completely there. What I was questioning was whether cinema really thought before that.

*JLG*: There was the idea that it was possible. When Welles made *Citizen Kane*, it was because it was still possible.

*YI*: In a way Welles also belongs to the afterwards. He too had the idea that something had been broken. He had a terrible fear of the possibility that fascism would spread, he'd written scripts about it that he wasn't allowed to shoot. There was the war too...

*JLG*: Even *Citizen Kane*?

*YI*: Yes, because cinema and society in the thirties were a sort of unanimism, consensus, American cinema most of all, and *Citizen Kane* is an anti-consensus film...

*JLG*: But it was in the Stroheim tradition, renewed, reinvented...

*YI*: Also in your film, since there's never anything on its own, on top of the images from *The Magnificent Ambersons* there's the overprint of a shot of Stroheim directing *Greed*, it's the idea of a Stroheim-Welles consanguinity and at the same time two destroyed films and two destroyed directors...

*JLG*: Welles was in the Ford tradition, he had the thoughts for Ford that Ford didn't have for himself...

*YI*: There, that's the difference exactly. I believe before everything that happened, before the Second World War, before the break that had occurred and that continued to widen until the point of no return of the camps, before all that the situation in cinema was that thought *was* form, then there came thought that was thought *about* form, and that's in Welles, to some extent in the Italians and a lot in you, thought about form. The difference between you and Hollywood cinema, like the very conscious and deliberate difference between Welles and Ford, is a difference from pure action cinema...

*JLG*: Let's say Welles still thought there were heaps of possibilities... My own view is that you could say broadly that it all stopped between 1940 and 1945, but it's more emblematic to say at Auschwitz. And actually people didn't really believe it at first, but there were individuals who thought or believed it...

*YI*: There was very little Auschwitz effect, at least consciously. Cinema only took it in much later, and perhaps never has absorbed it properly. In the immediate sense, the television-communications-media complex has had a much more seriously destructive effect on cinema and film makers than awareness of the impenetrable obstacle of the extermination camps, quite simply because that was buried, people didn't want to see it...

*JLG*: Absolutely...

*YI*: While what there is in your *Histoire(s)*, it's the way, by means of two quotations at the beginning of the last chapter, you state and define with extraordinary precision the overall aim of your film. Over the celebrated image of the Jewish child with hands raised, a child being deported or already in a camp, you say: "*I know now what voice it was that I might have wished to precede me*," and go on to say that you're speaking "*... in this place where I used to listen to him and where he himself is no longer present to hear me*"... It's plainly about the deed of speaking, about the right to speak, in all that that implies in terms of responsibility in relation to the other, before ethics and before History. But that leads straight into another quotation: "*oh, choosing the most solitary moment of nature let my whole and unique melody rise and swell on the evening air and do all that it can and say the thing that the thing is and fade and resume and cause vexation oh, solo of sobs...*" I believe that defines your film very well, with its aspects of the impossible and

76

of profound and melancholy solitude: the voice of the other in mine, and my melody in the universe...

*JLG*: The second text is a poem by Jules Laforgue, the first quote I took from Foucault...

*YI*: But you made them your own. In this last part one no longer distinguishes between you and the quotes, one can't tell whether the quotes are saying you or you're saying the quotes. Perhaps it's because it's you who are saying them, it's altogether different from the ones you had read or recited by others, actors or not, on camera or not, texts by Baudelaire, Broch, Élie Faure and so on, texts that are there, of course, for their content of thought on art or cinema, but also as records of the century. But here, in this last chapter, you're in a sort of complete symbiosis with your quotations. In this last part everything is said about film in the film itself; you could say the film's thought finds its full resonance there. If the other chapters are to a second power in relation to the history of cinema, here in the last it's more like a second power in relation to your *Histoire(s)*. The other parts had to be there before this summary and allusive totalization could give them a new resonance. We're in the realms of pure poetry, a sort of music, well beyond discursive reflection. I make no comparisons, but I'd mention Rilke's *Elegies* to give an idea of the order and level I'm talking about. But

77

arriving at that point, at the need to "say" yourself, that seems to me something new for you...

*JLG*: Let's say it's a feeling of drawing a sort of line under it, it's so that one can move on... I've always worked rather instinctively; I've made the films the situation dictated, as it were, or the ones I was capable of making, and I've also made films to earn a living. I'm still amazed that I've managed to earn a living with films for forty years...

*YI*: It's a rarity, especially in view of the films you've made, because of course other people get rich with other sorts of film... What's astonishing is that you've earned your living with the films you wanted to make...

*JLG*: ... the ones I could. I never say I want to make such and such a film, because every time I said that it was turned down. While I was making *Histoire(s)* at Gaumont I suggested five or six films to them, to absolutely no avail... When Benjamin wrote his book on passages it hadn't been commissioned by Gallimard...

*YI*: Benjamin started the book under very difficult conditions, almost utter destitution, and he left it unfinished because he committed suicide fleeing the Gestapo. But that's the difference between a book and a film, you can write a book or start one without a publisher, but for a film the first imperative need is money.

*JLG*: A painter can do it, cinema can't, there's a costliness threshold.

# 14

# *What Can Cinema Do?*

*YI*: So if there's the money handicap on top of all the rest, why is cinema privileged? Since you say, in connection with Nazism, that cinema ought to have ... that film-makers tried ... that they had warned, or when you say that in the darkened auditoriums the masses had been seething with the imaginary for fifty years and reality was now claiming its share of tears and blood... But you could say that it was the whole culture that had failed, not just cinema, it wasn't just a matter of cinema being privileged or being incapable...

*JLG*: All right, but cinema ought to have made it a point of honor... That also means I would have wanted to do it, or even today I ought to, but I won't, it means that too. I'd like to have done more, perhaps too ambitiously although that isn't the right word in this case...

**YI**: As you say, "*what is cinema*," compared to the horror of the real world? "*Nothing*," "*it wants the lot*" and "*it can do something*."

**JLG**: It's strange, in literature, with communism and Nazism, a lot of intellectuals wrote books, those books were published and read, and yet everyone carried on just the same... When Malraux and Gide went down to the Association they knew what was going on in Russia... And it's still like that today, when Jospin says he's happy with the outcome of the Pinochet affair, or condemns dictators while rushing off to shake pincers with Kabila or someone... It had all been said, all the German emigrés said it. You may think all those writers weren't big-circulation apart from Gide, and even Gide didn't have print runs of a million, it was for the intellectual milieu. While cinema had certain people of quality, more or less, like Renoir, Ford and Chaplin in particular, and they could have and it wasn't done. "Could do better" as they say, cinema was the favorite son, let's admit that it should have been first among the Cassandras and not a peep was heard. So I tell myself: there's something there. And then afterwards, books were published after the concentration camps. They couldn't be successful, understandably, but at least it had been done at last, while cinema still didn't do it and then when so-called Resistance films were made, and there were heaps of them, they were just spy thrillers and so on... Here too cinema had a second chance but didn't take it. That's why I quote the example of *Rome, Open City*, although it isn't quite there, although it's a bit fake, although Rossellini ... actually Roberto's prewar past is not without a murky side that needs closer examination. But there's a bizarre aspect: why Italy? Why not Greece? Why not France? Perhaps because Italy had lost its soul, France hadn't lost it but no longer knew where it was.

*YI*: Things were complicated in Greece, because after the Nazi occupation there was the destruction of the Communists so that the Tito story wouldn't be repeated, and it's that civil war, much more than fascism, that's still the repressed of Greek History. France's situation was very different, France had been occupied. French Resistance had consisted essentially of resistance to the occupier – "*the enemy*" to De Gaulle whom you quote in your film – rather than specific resistance to Nazism. While Italy had been a fascist country, indeed the first, and the Italians had mounted a resistance against themselves and their fascism... The reason why Italy is that the Italian republic dates from the Resistance. That shouldn't be forgotten. It was a new birth. You say Italian cinema is the identity of Italy, because Italy's new identity was formed at that time, formed in the Resistance.

*JLG*: In the French Resistance as it really was, they were all men and women. I'd rather say boys and girls because they were all very young. They all had lovers or sweethearts. None of that exists for historians; they don't mention it. You don't imagine things like that in daylight; only cinema could do it. There must have been betrayals, jealousies, stuff like that. But for historians none of that exists, so it's pretty weird history they write about… Basically it takes fifty years – I don't know about other periods but since the beginning of the twentieth century it's taken fifty years to start. You have to skip the children's generation and go to the grandchildren's. After that it's gone. If you don't do it then it's lost, forgotten, or else it's memorized, or sanctified. It's all been seen in France; France is quite exemplary in this matter. It's doing its work in this area with Jean Moulin, with Papon. It's doing its work, but the way it's doing it… it isn't very well done. There's the time factor: I started making films in '60, and there were a few years before that. In the year 2000 that will be exactly fifty years, just the right moment for me to take an interest in those stories. There's more time between my first film and my latest than there was for my father between the First and Second Wars, two-and-a-half times as long. When the time comes I can wonder: "*How did he see all that?*" Or when, for example, I read a historian who said that Pétain's

Latin teacher had been at Waterloo – when you read something like that, straight away there's all that time between Waterloo and '40... That time dimension, that's what cinema should devote itself to – properly made cinema. Even in documentary mode cinema can give that time scale that exists for everyone.

# 15

# *Only Cinema Narrates Large-scale History by Narrating its Own History*

*YI*: Only cinema can narrate History with a capital H simply by telling its own history, the other arts can't.

*JLG*: Because it's made from the same raw material as History. The fact is that even when it's recounting a slight Italian or French comedy, cinema is much more the image of the century in all its aspects than some little novel; it's the century's metaphor. In relation to History, the most trivial clinch or pistol shot in cinema is more metaphorical than anything literary. Its raw material is metaphorical in itself. Its reality is already metaphorical. It's an image on the scale of the man in the street, not the infinitely small atomic scale or the infinitely huge galactic one. What it has filmed most is men and women of average age. In a place where it is in the living present, cinema addresses them simply: it reports them, it's the registrar of History. It could be the registrar, and if the right scientific research were done afterwards it would be a social support; it wouldn't neglect the social side.

*YI*: Cinema has this archive aspect because it's about recording. That's why, you say, there ought to be equality and fraternity between reality and fiction in cinema. Because it's both things together, cinema can bear witness. Even independently of the war news, a simple 35 mm rectangle saves the honor of reality, you say; every film is a news document. Cinema only films the past, meaning what passes. It is memory and the refuge of time. Because of this recording apect there's a relationship between photography or cinema and History that doesn't exist elsewhere. Cinema has this dimension of historicity that the other arts don't have. That's why, as you have said, even a fiction film is metaphorical in relation to History, because it's a trace of the outside... This was the case even if films were unaware of it, until it becomes obvious...

*JLG*: Quite a bit of time has passed...

*YI*: We were talking earlier about using transparencies and tricks of that sort. I think that was a case of reality being canned in advance to be projected on set

and incorporated into a fictional world. In that way
History, or the real world, was taken metaphorically
inside fiction, while you took fiction into the real
world. You recall it by saying, apropos the Nouvelle
Vague, that you wanted the right to film boys and
girls in a real world in such a way that when they saw
the film they would be astonished to be themselves
and in the world. Even more than Truffaut or Rivette,
it seems to me that ever since *À bout de souffle* you've
been violently exposing the fiction outside. To cite
an idea of Benjamin, we've moved from a magical
value of cinema to a value of exposure, the historicity
that is an effect of technical reproduction. And from
that starting point what you showed in *Histoire(s)* was
all the historicity of cinema, not just as a historical
record, all those images and sounds you took from
newsreels, but also the metaphorical dimension of
fictional cinema in relation to History. By insisting on
the fact that these relations work in both directions,
not just that History altered the destiny of cinema
or that cinema as such had an effect on History, but
that this reciprocity between cinema and History can
be seen in very specific images, as in the case of *Ivan
the Terrible* and Stalin, or by quoting what Bazin had
written on Chaplin and Hitler...

*JLG*: I put that in, I showed how Hitler had stolen his
moustache...

*YT:* Of course there's that overprint and meta-morphosis, but that's not all there is. It's not just Hitler's theft of Chaplin's moustache. In that overprint there appears the idea of the presence in man of the "Other." Chaplin in a way is the emblematic figure of cinema. Your film starts with him; he's also one of the last figures to appear with Keaton, when you're talking about the end of cinema. But he's a constant presence throughout the film. Chaplin's Little Fellow is the emblematic character of cinema, also in a way a figure for the decent man, the man who doesn't aspire to power and hasn't got any, but at the same time through the fade-out/fade-in the Other appears from underneath, absolute horror or Hitler, not from the outside but from within the same humanity. That Other also has its emblematic figure in cinema and in your film: Nosferatu. Thus in relation to Hisory there's something that appears with a sort of permanence, among other things in the repeated clips from *Alexander Nevsky* and the Teutonic knights massacring people, which is the horror characteristic of the twentieth century, whose most extreme manifestation is Nazism. Thus among a hundred examples, that of the wolf running through the desert shot dead from a helicopter, with voiceover describing the death of an unconscious woman buried alive by murderers who haven't even finished her off. But when you're talking about the camera not having changed for a long time, you show Gide's nephew's film on Africa, Captain Blood and his cannon, Mussolini and the crowd and Mussolini behind a camera. Looking at *Histoire(s)*, the first chapter especially, I got the impression there had been three major events in the twentieth century: the Russian revolution, Nazism and cinema, particularly Hollywood cinema, which is the power of cinema, the plague as you say.

*JLG*: People usually mention the first two, the Russian revolution and Nazism, but not the third, which is cinema.

*YI*: Of course the effects weren't the same, these three events are not comparable, but they coexist and determine the century. You even make some of those juxtapositions of widely different things producing a violent shock effect: an advertisement for an American porn video following the image of Lenin's motheaten mummy; or when the question is raised of American cinema having destroyed the European cinemas, over the image of Max Linder with a caption reading "*help me*," his last words, the voiceover is a woman's voice saying how long it takes to die in a gas chamber ...

*JLG*: That's a matter of interpretation, because in me there's no idea of interpretation. But people often say you shouldn't make an amalgam, it isn't a question of amalgam, the things are set down together, the conclusion isn't given straight away, people ought to be stretched... There's projection, that depends on the feelings people have, and Conrad says feelings are the handmaids of our passions...

*YI*: Of course, the film isn't linear or a discourse in the indicative, it's not a matter of cause and effect, or of comparison, let alone identification. There's contiguity because things existed together.

*JLG*: They existed together, so one recalls that they existed together.

*YI*: The importance you attribute to cinema, by saying specifically that the masses love myth and cinema is addressed to the masses, far outweighs the compliment usually paid to cinema, that it's the major art form created in the twentieth century. The power referred to is one that far outweighs the question of art and is indeed a historic force, full stop. Perhaps one of the differences between the Soviet Union, Germany and the United States is that the first two didn't have and couldn't have what Hollywood represented for American history. Because people are beginning to realize, in America at least, that modern big-city America and the absorption of the immigrant masses in the late nineteenth and early twentieth centuries was achieved as a result of the American dream created by Hollywood, with a weekly audience in its heyday of a hundred million people. That cinema also made the power of America abroad, its conquest of the world since the Second World War being due not only to military, technical and economic supremacy but also to the power of its cinema. There was a dream factory that conquered the world and then there was the "utopia" of the Russian revolution which turned into a nightmare represented, with all that implies, by Lenin's obscene disintegrating mummy, by the fact of its exhibition...

*JLG*: Even Lenin's idea of communism wasn't the same as Marx's...

*YI*: What people forget is that Russia and its history existed in the background...

*JLG*: There's communism and then there are communists. The history of Russia isn't written, and it's really a pity from the historians' point of view. Even when Furet[1] does the history of the Revolution there are images, there's a mode of thought. When he does the history of Russia they're no longer there, there's text and not even overtext, as Péguy called it, but undertext, and despite the astonishing number of images that exist and that are starting to be seen today, Furet didn't even see a Russian peasant in an

Eisenstein film. There was a sequence I wanted to do in *The Old Place* but didn't because of falling back into *Histoire(s) du cinéma*, I wanted to juxtapose two photos of corpses and say: "this one died in Russia and this one in Germany, where's the difference, where's the absence of difference?" I don't find the same thing in fascism and communism... I'm not going to advance, you could call them hypotheses, or argue with someone by saying what you assert when you say that the evil was in communism, you should think it through, do further research, instead of all these ideological disputes which aren't a quest for truth, while the images are there. So this is the place to say that where cinema tripped over itself was with this obligation to see: it didn't know, it wouldn't, it couldn't, anyway it didn't at the time of Nazism. The obligation to resist, there's one film that did it knowingly – *Rome, Open City* – and after that it vanished. Nothing forced Roberto to make that film...

*YI*: It's because there was that moment of History in Italy and at that moment there was a favorable situation: cinema tells stories that have a metaphorical relation with History, but here History was a presence in the street, and Rossellini shot the movie in the streets. You say yourself it's not just a resistance film, it's a film that resists the uniform way of making cinema.

*JLG*: That's why I said out of uniform, because Capra's films aren't like that but on the contrary are made to give America an all-conquering image. Because America needed to dominate the world bit by bit and used cinema, or cinema very consciously and politically volunteered to be used, and because that became customary and Europe accepted it...

*YI*: Getting back to this permanence of horror...

*JLG*: It's a matter of copying. It isn't just painters who made copies to learn, when they used to go to Italy to copy a Raphael, they didn't do a hundred, they made one copy, it's creation...

*YI*: It's Benjamin's idea about technical reproducibility...

*JLG*: From the moment it could be done technically, when cinema had the means to show its products by running off a number of copies, it also brought in the idea of copying on a larger scale. Since then, when horror is copied it's copied several times, so there aren't just the trenches of 1914 but there's Sarajevo, Rwanda, the Spanish Civil War. There's a lot more of it, you could say horror's being exploited, and that's the moment when the means of pure diffusion arrives, not even copying, just diffusion, and that's TV, and it's even going to be reproduced in cinema, since copies aren't even going to be made any more, films will be exploited by satellite instead. In other words there's going to be pure diffusion, production in the name of diffusion... The twentieth century exploited that, there was more war, more horror... horror had to be democratized too, so to speak...

*YI*: In all your references to painting there's one painter who is always there and that's Goya, for example when you quote the Hugo text. Goya is a painter who painted the horror of humanity, quite simply, horror without redemption...

*JLG*: I'd never seen any Goya paintings, I went to see them once in the Prado, I was very disoriented, I didn't find what Malraux said at all ... there are some very strange figures...

## *Note*

1. François Furet (1927–97), French historian. A communist in youth, helped found PSU (Socialist Party) in 1960. A major writer on the French Revolution and subsequent French republican and monarchist politics, in 1995 published *Le Passé d'une illusion: essai sur l'idée du communisme au XXe siècle*, a self-critical reflection on the wilful blindness of intellectuals towards Soviet reality.

# 16

# *In Cinema as in Christianity: Image and Resurrection*

**YI**: In Goya there's the absolute of horror, and then the beauty of women. But even there one finds what you say about fatal beauty and sorcery through the ages: promise, seduction and destruction. It isn't really redemption, since you put an overprint of Goya's beauties on a balcony over an image of a camp charnelhouse. To generalized horror as a condition of the world, myth replies with beauty. In your film although there's the mythical – because permanent and unavoidable – dimension of horror and fatal beauty, this dimension seems to find its redemption in art or Christianity, which you might say was the same thing. Because when the orchestra in the camps is mentioned, you say that art is born from what has been burned and you superimpose on the image of the camp Grünewald's Virgin and Child. It's an explicit identification of art with the birth of Christ. And it's a constant from beginning to end. At another point, two nuns from *Les Anges du péché* appear, through overprinting, to be genuflecting on either side of a railway line leading to the gate of an extermination camp seen in long shot. There's also, with Grünewald, Monet's *Rising Sun* and a little later the first 16mm colour film shot by George Stevens at Auschwitz, leading on to Elizabeth Taylor and her happiness finding a place in the sun. Which could be deeply shocking to a Jew who might see it as representing the appropriation of the unavoidable, the absolutely nameless and unrepresentable, by Christianity or some artist's metaphysics... Although there's still the unbeliever Goya, with his images of horror and disaster, or his Saturn, time eating its children, or his knife-wielding Judith, there's also the constant presence of Rembrandt, a Christian painter if there ever was one, you liken the screen to the Samaritan's cloak or to a shroud, and there's a Rembrandt deposition from the cross with Christ's body and the winding-sheet. So Christianity seems to be the main thing...

*JLG*: That's History. I recall Christianity as the first film, it's there in all painters, it's something literature hasn't done.

*YI*: Of course it's because of the image of Christ and its more or less liturgical function… But we could return to *La Mort de Virgile*, which Broch had started to write when he was interned, despite his conversion to Protestantism, in a camp from which he was saved with great difficulty. I read this book ages ago, but from what I remember Virgil wants to burn his writings because, given the horror and obscenity of the world, "*beauty is a form of slumber*," because he thought that beauty as it was conceived could no longer redeem any part of this world, that's why he seems to announce another form of redemption identified with Christ. Were you concerned with any of this in your film?

*JLG*: No, just bits and pieces with me… Sometimes when I spoke of Christianity, it's not from belief, it's as a historical phenomenon, as a movement of thought. And when once I quote the Malraux text that says that if myth begins with Fantômas it ends with Christ, I'm quoting Malraux's text called *La Psychologie du cinéma*, which is one of his first writings on the psychology of art…

*YI*: Over the image of a bomb falling; an image that ends with a white spectral form like a skull. In your film there's never just one image or just one idea, there are resonances, but also the opposite. Thus over the image of Christ, of Pasolini, when it might seem that here is the truth to which you are drawn, there's a caption with two film titles: *Bitter Victory* and *Rebel Without a Cause*, so that the promise of Christ becomes something not kept. Something that also seems very central to the film is the quotation, often repeated, that you took from St Paul: "*The image will come at the time of resurrection . . .*" An idea you even back up with another quotation – over images from *Vertigo* and *Pandora*, films about death and resurrection – when there's the reflection on whether the dead Christ was a man or an image, and whether a filmed man is a man or already the fiction of a man (J.L. Schefer), which links with your phrase "*in cinema as in Christianity.*"

*JLG*: In relation to painting and photography, Christianity made such a fuss about image, compared to other civilizations, which saw the question of whether to paint the Buddha as neither here nor there . . .

*YI*: It's for a very simple reason, because Christianity emerged from Judaism which had forbidden the human image as idolatry, because in other religions there was a relation between image and the gods while in Judaism God is unrepresentable . . .

*JLG*: That's quite important really, because if there was an image of God then people would see it and the whole thing would collapse . . . like Dubillard when he said "*I saw the Void once, and there's a lot less to it than people think...*"

*YI*: There isn't just the recurrence of the phrase saying that "*the image will come at the time of resurrection*" or "*the image is of the order of redemption*" accompanied by Piero's or d'Angelico's Christ or Piero's angel with the dead man from Lascaux or a body from *Octobre à Paris*, one gets the feeling that cinema ought to have been a sort of second coming of Christ...

*JLG*: Not at all. Something was invented and not properly used, something no one knew how to use or wanted to use.

*YI*: And at that moment, perhaps there's the promise of resurrection, like a sacral creation story, fall, revelation, confirmation and resurrection... In this connection I remember a conversation between you and Sollers concerning *Je vous salue Marie*, when you mentioned the creation of the world by a bad God.

*JLG*: Yes I remember that, I quoted that story in *Hélas pour moi*, it's something someone had told me...

*YI*: It's the gnostic concept of the bad demiurge who rushed to create the world in order to thwart the real God. With the good God there really are only images, there's the astral body, nothing material, no sexuality or reproduction, all that is the effect of the bad demiurge, but there do exist a few sparks of light, the promise of that return to the astral body and the world of the image, which appear from time to time in beauty. For in your film sexuality is redeemed by the invisible part, that is by love; its visible part consists essentially of pornographic images, which you often superimpose on images of horror from the camps, rather shockingly, and I must say it shocked me. The Gnostics also have the idea that what is purely earthly and thus part of the profane world should be burned, it's in the fire of the spirit that the spirit reveals itself, a bit like what you say about art being like fire and being born out of what it burns. In the context of what you see as the degradation of cinema by evil, money, pornography and violence, what you call the absence of thought that abandons us to brutality, isn't it possible that when you show a corpse being thrown into a mass grave in the camps you're straying into the same territory?

*JLG*: No, it's simply that people don't know how to use cinema. Even pornography could be made differently if people knew how to use it; perhaps that shouldn't be shown, there's a temptation but people don't know, I don't know, something everyone loves... There's a quote from St. Augustine that I wanted to put in the film and then forgot: something like "*Men so love the truth that those who tell it not yearn for what they tell to be the truth.*" It should have been done ...

*YI*: Cinema should have been made, but very little has been, that's the problem ...

*JLG*: There's been a lot, but very little actually, it was very young ... Texts come from longer ago, and anyway the first texts were about money, the earliest tablets ... it was accountancy. By contrast the earliest images had nothing to do with bookkeeping ... An image is peaceable. An image of the Virgin and her baby on a donkey doesn't cause a war; its interpretation by a text is what will lead to war and cause Luther's soldiers to go and deface Raphael canvases. I have a strong feeling that the image enables us to talk less and say more.

*YI*: To you words are enemies.

*JLG*: No, only when they're taken as orders, or thoughtless, or used malevolently as weapons.

*YI*: When you talk about life being fullness in itself, irreducible completeness in every sense, the starting point for the other is established by pronouncing the word man (M. Kacem). And from the moment there is man, the other appears. You could say words were a bit like that, it's why you also say that cinema showed, that cinema told stories without telling them.

*JLG*: There's a mystery all the same, because it started as silent cinema and for thirty years there was no reason for it to be silent; it could have had sound but it had started silent, then was like a child who's been perverted. Anyway that's more or less how I see it, but there's nevertheless what's called a historical fact. You'd have to find ... for example the invention of the script, I say it was a Mafia accountant, it's an intuition but one that ought to be checkable. Since the invention of the script is getting something under control, you can imagine something of that sort would have happened, not exactly that but something like it, especially as we know the Mafia moved from New York to Los Angeles the moment Hollywood was born... When I say it's a small-time Mafia accountant...

# 17

# *Image and Montage*

**YI**: That's the sort of juxtaposition...

**JLG**: That's it, it's a juxtaposition and it's an image, like many of the ones in *Histoire(s)*. No one but me has said that at one point in the extermination camps the Germans had decided to declare a Jew to be a Muslim. Although they all knew it, the survivors, it's in all the books, but no one made the juxtaposition, not even when war broke out in the Middle East... But that's an image, one day it struck me as an image, that there should be two words juxtaposed, it's two images...

**YI**: When you quote the text from Blanchot saying the image is well-being ... despite the reference to well-being, with Blanchot the image doesn't seem to have the immediate fullness that you usually give it, it's primarily associated with the Void.

**JLG**: He says image is gaze...

*YI*: The gaze of the Void on us...

*JLG*: It's hard to think that image is gaze, because we still think image is gaze but through the lens...

*YI*: But here it's the images that are looking at us, that's why it's our absence, it's the absence we see there and it's the gaze of the Void on us... And here I think that in the conclusion of your film, it's this relation between the Void and the beneficence of the image and art that matters, and it's a different conception from the Christian one...

*JLG*: Yes, absolutely... When Blanchot says image is well-being, people talk to you about well-being too, they want to be happy. If it's too literary it gets forgotten. When it's said that image is well-being, no one except me immediately envisages someone laughing or crying, but I do. It's a difference that hinders me from talking to people afterwards, because we don't function in the same way. I function to excess in some areas and I have the impression of talking to people who don't, whose surplus is somewhere else entirely.

*YI*: It's terrible to have the gift of feeling everything with such intensity, you quote Virginia Woolf as saying. You think, feel and see in image, while others pay more attention to what you call meaning, text or ideas or concepts, which don't much enjoy your favor. Seeing, feeling, thinking in images isn't just being a film maker; it's having a vision and an essentially poetic practice of cinema, in contrast to those who want to communicate meaning, to make dramas, stories or romances. To return once more to Eisenstein's idea, on the level of detail and as a whole, your film isn't attempting to represent a theme but the image of a theme, and that's the main difference from other people's work. The image being the metaphorical and affective resonances, harmonics and counterpoint that create the Idea rather than just communicating facts. Nevertheless, despite the constant presence of Eisenstein as the master of montage, your concept of montage seems to me to have a different inflection. For in Eisenstein, through what he calls the dialectics of nature, there's still the idea of the organic work of art, a whole that is accomplished by going outside the self in a series of successive leaps and explosions, while *Histoire(s) du cinéma*, in detail as well as overall, is formed out of more or less large units in a non-organic relation with the central ideas. There's no nucleus from which all the rest could be deduced by development, since what's being done is a constant assimilation of new ideas or facts into an extremely mobile composition. Your conception of the cinema image as that which shows, as revelation, fullness before interpretation, redemption and resurrection of the real, is very close to Bazin, and at the same time montage is your "big concern," as it was Eisenstein's. From beginning to end of your *Histoire(s)* the editing console is seen as a machine for exploring time, but it's only at the end, over the recurrent image of Eisenstein – over which there's the caption juxtaposing Israel Ismael, the Muslim German Jew, with the image of Mabuse and the two soldiers dragging a corpse in a camp – that you quote Reverdy's text and the idea of the image as the specific meeting of two unconnected things, it's also where we see, just this once, your hands bringing two pieces of film together, and it's in this context that you show images of André Bazin with the caption: "montage forbidden." Here as throughout the film you work with positive and negative, with opposites at the same time. Another thing you say is that all that remains of films in the memory is images, and on this level, in your film, all the images of cinema are co-present as time transformed into the timeless by art, and here there's no history strictly speaking, as there is by contrast in History, which isn't art but the changing reign of Saturn and of time.

*JLG*: This relation between positive and negative, which was expounded by Hegel, existed in cinema on the simplest material level. Cinema is the image of it, but with digital the negative disappears, there's no more negative and positive but a sort of flat linearity, the contradictory relation between day and night no longer exists, it took a century to disappear. Which leads me to say at one point that cinema is a nineteenth-century idea that took a century to become a reality and disappear. Which means that the twentieth century didn't invent much, enabling me to exaggerate a bit, but it's only an image, by saying that the twentieth century by itself didn't exist much: it didn't invent horror, it just churned out thousands of copies. It had few ideas: relativity, quantum mechanics, all that comes from the nineteenth. Reactionary thinkers were quick to say that the twentieth century saw the rise of technology, of the ideology of technology, but technology was invented in the nineteenth century. There were applications; there was no invention.

# 18

# Towards the Stars

**YI**: The end of the century and of art is addressed again in *The Old Place*, which you made for the city of New York Museum of Modern Art. But that film is separate from *Histoire(s)* owing to the vigilance of Anne-Marie Miéville, even though it sometimes mines the same ore. *Histoire(s) du cinéma* is a sort of closure on a cinema that had been one of the major forces of the twentieth century, and that also created forms. Seeing *Histoire(s)*, one has the impression that this cinema or this function of cinema has ended. While by contrast, doubtless as a result of your collaboration with Anne-Marie Miéville, *The Old Place* is a sort of opening on what is still possible. It ends neverthelss with the image of Charlie Chaplin and Paulette Goddard walking on either side of what could be the line of a frontier. But it's a projection, not this time into the past, in quest of a territory and motherland that no longer exist, but towards the future and the stars.

*JLG*: Absolutely, exactly. We have to feel a bit like that, or we'd commit suicide. There's no such thing as reason. Thinking, creating, is an act of resistance; that's what Deleuze was saying in his fashion. It was to get through on the level of understanding, to be understood in the raw sense and the intuitive one. So that people leave thinking: "goodness, that's how it is." But for me *Histoire(s) du cinéma* was historical, it wasn't despairing at all. It shows things that induce despair. There's a fair amount to be despairing about, but existence can't despair. We can say broadly that a certain idea of cinema which wasn't Lumière's but was perhaps Feuillade's up to a point – which continued with Delluc and Vigo, and which I myself feel quite close to – that idea of cinema has passed, as the Fontainebleau School passed, as Italian painting passed, as very suddenly – Braudel gives a good account of this – Venice gave place to Amsterdam and then Amsterdam to Genoa and then Genoa to London and then New York. You could say that a certain cinema is now concluded. As Hegel said, an epoch has ended. Afterwards things are different. One feels sad because childhood has been lost. But it's normal too. Now there's a new cinema, and a different art, whose history will be made in fifty or a hundred years. Now humanity's in a new chapter, and perhaps even the idea of History will change.

*Part II*
*Jean-Luc Godard*
*Cinéaste of Modern Life:*
*The Poetic in the Historical*
*By Youssef Ishaghpour*

Baudelaire's *Le Peintre de la vie moderne* may not be the first manifestation of aesthetic modernity but is surely one of its earlier formulations. Because by thinking about the relation between the historical and the eternal in art, it introduces the dimension of historicity, of actuality.

"This is a fine opportunity, in truth," Baudelaire writes

to establish a rational and historical theory of the beautiful, in opposition to the theory of beauty as single and absolute; to show that beauty is always, inevitably, of dual composition, even though it produces a single impression; for the difficulty of separating the variable elements of the beautiful from the impression of unity in no way reduces the need for variety in composing it. The beautiful is made up of an unvarying eternal element, whose quantity is excessively difficult to determine, and a relative, circumstantial element arising from the epoch, from fashion, morality or passion, one at a time or all at once. Without this second element, as it were the attractive, titillating, appetizing container for the divine cake, the first element would be indigestible, unpalatable, ill-adapted and inappropriate to human nature.

A few pages later Baudelaire adds that the task with modernity "is ... to separate out from the current fashion whatever it may contain of the poetic in the historical, to draw the eternal out of the transitory."[1]

This text has sometimes been taken in a reductive sense that wipes out its original intuition. For if the historical is defined only by the envelope containing something that might be eternal in itself, it becomes impossible to see what differentiates Renaissance painting – whose principle was to use the present as an envelope for the eternal forms of Beauty, meaning classical Antiquity – from modern painting, whose essence is marked by historicity and its opposition to anything that might be eternal, but not to a present rendered "timeless" by its metamorphosis through art. It has sometimes been thought that this relation between the historical and the eternal was just a simple matter of redemption of the ephemeral and current element in the eternal world of the idea, without the need for any change in art's attitude to the present. Baudelaire himself seems to have leaned heavily in this direction, and he often snubbed contemporary work that was more or less radically new, including Courbet's work along with Manet's.[2]

The break that made a problem of the relationship between the historical and the timeless came in 1848, with the eruption onto the world stage of "historicity": a conflict-ridden present charged with utopia or virtuality. To appreciate the nature of the change one need only recall that the French Revolution had arrived in the world draped in the garb of Antiquity: 1848, especially during the days of June, saw a radical break with the past, along with what Courbet (in another context) called "the burial of romanticism."[3] That, combined with the development of technological means of reproduction – the mass-market press reducing History to a factual, explainable present,[4] and photography reducing the world to what the camera sees and records[5] – silenced the former eloquence.[6] These three developments – awareness of historicity, technical means of reproduction and the disappearance of the former eloquence – gave birth to modern art and literature. And the same elements are still there in Godard's cinema, in another situation and with different modalities.

"The duality of art," Baudelaire writes

is an inevitable consequence of the duality of man.
Consider, if you will, the eternal and unchanging part
as the soul of art, and the variable element as its body.
That is why Stendhal ... came closer to the truth than
many others by saying that *the Beautiful is nothing but
the promise of happiness.* No doubt this definition misses
the target; it subordinates the beautiful too broadly
to the infinitely variable ideal of happiness; it divests
the beautiful too readily of its aristocratic character;
but it has the great merit of distancing itself from the
error of the academicians.[7]

What matters here is not Baudelaire's idea of
the duality between body and soul as analogous to
the duality between the variable and unchanging
elements in art, but the reference to Stendhal's idea
and the inflection Baudelaire gives it: if the Beautiful
is nothing but the promise of happiness, then it must
metamorphose along with "the infinitely variable
ideal of happiness." Regarding the beautiful not as
a reality but as a promise is hardly new. We find it in
slightly different form even in Aristotle, who defined
the poetic as "what might be" in contrast to the
historical, which relates "what has been." The novelty
in Baudelaire's observation lies in his introduction
of the historical into the poetic, by recognizing
the inevitability of change in perceptions of the
beautiful.

What Baudelaire's text was driving at on relations
between the poetic and the historical had earlier
been central to the thinking of the first German
romantics at Jena.[8] For the univocal definition of the
Beautiful, which Baudelaire rejects as "the error of
the academicians," corresponded with traditional
aesthetics in holding the idea of the beautiful, as
the sole aim of art, to be something eternal, and
excluding from the art domain everything that did
not meet a standard defined once and for all. But
during the decline of the Classical Age, as it became
clear that the Middle Ages were important as well
as ancient Greece, that Shakespeare or Cervantes
could be considered on the same level as Sophocles,
people were forced to admit the historical diversity
of forms and the intrinsic connection between art
and time. It was no longer a question of finding
eternity in different forms, but of seeing form as a
means of making the newness and strangeness of the
moment into something timeless, thus redeeming
the temporal and saving the ephemera of life with its
unkept promise. There is thus a shift from the idea
of the Beautiful to the idea of the Poetic as such; to
the idea of Art in itself, which henceforth replaces
the idea of the Beautiful as the aim and main object
of works of art, something that can be seen again
in Godard's work. That is how the poetic, the idea
of Art, became the Organon of the Absolute, since

religion had lost its hegemonic position and Kant had excluded the experience of the Absolute from philosophy, while reintroducing it, in provisional mode, in aesthetics, making possible if not a synthesis at least a contact between the palpable and the intelligible, the phenomenon and the idea, the finite and the infinite: all formulations of the duality pointed out by Baudelaire.

However, the recognition of duality, instead of leading to a synthesis of the poetic and the historical, becomes a source of problems. It determines those dimensions of reflexiveness and criticism – in the sense of questioning art and the possibility of art, and of criticizing the limits of reality – which are essential to modern art and a constant in Godard's work. The poetic, posed as an absolute, is seen as that which exposes the utopian tendencies and blind alleys of the historical, but always comes up against its own limitations, its absence of foundation and legitimacy, and can only be accomplished in fragmentary fashion, broken forms, fiction and reflection interwoven with humor and flashes of genius, the Artist's touch as found in Godard's work.

Returning from these ideas of the Jena romantics to Baudelaire and the mixture of ephemeral and eternal that he attributes to all forms of beauty, but not wishing to see the eternal as something fixed or outside time, one could perhaps see art as containing a sort of alchemy or mystique able to redeem the temporal into the timeless through metamorphosis. For although thought about time had existed in the Christian tradition since St. Augustine, time was not made into an absolute condition of thought until Kant, or an absolute of History until the French Revolution; and because it only became the horizon of existence as historicity after 1848, time not only destroyed the univocal and eternal meaning of beauty but bound the poetic and the historical together, at the same time setting them radically at odds.

For historicity is anti-poetic on at least two levels. One is the tendency of modernity in general, including artistic modernity, to focus increasingly on the present, and this is what is at work in Godard. This modern focus on the present is determined among other things by the existence of technical means of reproduction, now triumphant with the establishment of a planetary closed circuit of image-communications-merchandise functioning in real time. Which liquidates not only the poetic but the historical too: in real time the present is no longer recognized, no longer sought; the poetic possibility – achieved once again despite everything by Godard – of seeing it as more than it is in order to see it fully for what it is, has gone. There is no longer a present, just a perpetual disappearance that never joins the past. "The true face of history," Benjamin

121

wrote, "recedes at a gallop. The past is retained only as an image which, at the moment it allows itself to be recognized, casts a light that will never be seen again."[9]

The other level concerns the very essence of our History, of what makes the continuity of the chain of events, to quote Benjamin again, "one single catastrophe, endlessly piling ruins upon ruins and throwing them" at the feet of the Angel of History,[10] causing the Angel to stare and fall silent. Hence the insurmountable difficulty, not to say radical impossibility, of the poetic faced with this growing mountain of horrors and ruins. But in the words of another poet, Wallace Stevens, the poetic is "the necessary Angel."[11] It is something that cannot adapt either to the given or to any official concept of being. It is the possibility of conferring singularity on fragments of flux pure and simple. It is the ability to feel both the crushing weight of the world and our own power to help lift that weight, to deliver us from it. That feeling of liberation is the essential thing: it takes the necessary but unreal and risky form of an ironic or even gratuitous game, a way of defying the real world and the seriousness of art at the same time. The poetic aiming not to designate or define things but to extract their resonances, to expose to view and understanding the resonance between what is accessible and the underlying whole. It is this particular relation between the poetic and the historical that informs Godard's art, with the accent obviously on the poetic, on a poet's posture, but in the sense defined by the Jena romantics implying critical reflection and humour. This immediately distinguishes Godard – even when he is telling stories – from his old *Cahiers du cinéma* friends like Rivette, Rohmer and Truffaut, all more attached to the romantic, to stories or dramas.

"The utopianism of modern art," Meschonic said, had the function of "redeeming the hell of modernity." It consisted essentially of the metamorphosis of forms of expression; and historicity in these, such as it was, mainly concerned the historicity of the raw material. Not only because "art for art's sake" needed to respond, word for word as Hermann Broch remarked, to "business is business," which was starting to dominate the real world, but also because reality had been reduced in the same process to the shifting, ephemeral, anti-poetic, explainable and meaningless artificiality of facts and documents, photographically reproducible and transmissible by the mass-market press and information industry. All of this is to be found at the pivotal points of cinema, and not only Godard's cinema: one need only recall the negative function of "cinema newsreels," technical reproduction joined with information, in *Citizen Kane*, a negative function that serves by contrast to affirm the necessity and absolute value of works of art.

However, born of an awareness of historicity and achieved as it were in spite of it, art as an absolute – which tends to be transformed into a "religion of art" – is constantly exposed to historicity itself, which presses for the destruction of the unreality of art as a separate sphere. In two different ways. Either the horrors of History and the contrast between tradition and new images and techniques produce anti-art, by carrying irony and destructive humor into the very foundations of art; or History itself seems charged with utopian virtualities, leading to a wish to go beyond art as something absolute, unreal and separate, to eliminate the duality of the poetic and the historical by combining them in a militant, political art. Art as an absolute, anti-art and militant art: all three relations of the poetic to the historical are found to different extents and especially at different historical moments in the cinema of Godard, who like many modern artists works "in between" and functions in the gap, the interval, not just between images but between art and life, between the historical and the poetic.

Modernity being a tendency to reduce everything to the present, to the observable and reproducible, to what appears in front of or is determined by the camera, and modern art by contrast embodying

124

resistance to this reductive tendency by attempting to liberate its utopian virtualities, cinema, situated at the meeting point of these two possibilities, ought to be the most important thing in contemporary art. It certainly is that, or has been, but as the "factory of the century," as a mythical and magical force. For a start, the cinecamera should not be regarded as a simple means of reproducing reality, assuming it is still known what reality is and, more importantly, that it can be seen by the camera. In any case, when the image of reality is mentioned the "image" proper is always forgotten. Now whether it is a cave painting, an Egyptian statue of Ka, the Colossus of Rhodes, an image in a mirror or an image on the screen, there is always some sort of magical dimension in the image related to desire, to death, to shadows, to doubles, to immortality. In this connection, Edgar Morin's *Le cinéma ou l'homme imaginaire*[12] is the best book on the anthropological power of cinema. It is no accident that almost immediately after Lumière, Meliès arrived to make the magic of the image emerge from the image of reality. And here too Godard places himself in the gap of a perpetual questioning of these terms and the relation, inside the image, between the image of reality and the reality of image.

This magical dimension of the cinema image, greatly strengthened by its appearance of reality, is what gives cinema its extraordinary, fabulous power. But to understand the reasons for this power we need to look at the conditions prevailing at the birth of modern art. Earlier we mentioned two determining factors: awareness of historicity (resistance to "givens"), and the existence of technical means of reproduction. We mentioned in passing the importance of the new slogan "business is business." This needs to be emphasized, along with the predominance of the market, the rise of industrial production and the related appearance of anonymous masses in the great cities. By asserting its autonomy and total freedom, by regarding only the handling of raw material and the form of expression as genuinely artistic, modern art has defined itself by its resistance to the market, to the technical means of reproduction, and consequently to the public. In the process it had to distance itself from everything immediately consumable and communicable, whether in the order of image, fiction or emotion, consigning everything of that sort including the old ideas of the esthetic and the beautiful to the domain of kitsch, which had appeared at the same time as modern art: industrial output of a new merchandise, cultural goods for the masses. And it is precisely all that, the presence of anonymous masses in the great cities, the possibility of industrial reproduction, the market for kitsch and its modes of expression, that underlies the power of cinema as the dream of a dreamless world and the promise of joy and prodigy, of the "fatal beauty" that cinema inherited from the opera it had destroyed and supplanted.[13]

By asserting its creative and formal freedom modern art became an austere field for artists, connoisseurs and the elite, losing the community role it once had (largely destroyed in any case by post-1848 historical reality). That is why in the 1920s Élie Faure, and others too, envisaged cinema as the cathedral of the future, able to reconcile the public with the creative formal freedom of modern art in a new historical situation. With the cathedral becoming more and more like a supermarket a film maker like Godard, still committed to the idea of art and the role of cinema, inevitably found himself in the modern artist's stance of resistance to the specific conditions prevailing in cinema, with all that implies in terms of raw material, forms of expression and relations with the market, money and the public.

Since the power of cinema has been exploited essentially by the culture industry in the service of capital or the State, this relation between the poetic and the historical is not recognized as belonging more to cinema than any other art (cinema alone being a modern invention in the full sense of the word). It is not recognized, except in times of exceptional crisis when historicity as such – of the cinematic raw material as well as the historical moment – has closed in: Russia in the 1920s with Vertov and Eisenstein, during the Second World War with Welles and Rossellini, the crisis conditions caused by the Algerian War with the French Nouvelle Vague.

Godard's intermittent hostility to Eisenstein – at moments when he is carried away by the idea of construction, art as an absolute, or indeed the wish for deconstruction and openness to the outside – stems from the fact that in Eisenstein the raw material, well thought out in its specificities, is nevertheless reintegrated with the secular powers of art, themselves reinterpreted according to a dialectical general conception of image and montage; in the same way that the present moment is conceived as a historical event in an evolving History imbued with meaning. While Vertov – whose films seem to have inspired Walter Benjamin's text on technical reproduction and loss of aura – radically asserted the absolute novelty of the cinematic raw material, beyond script, or art, or History as meaning, in a sort of replay of the creation of the world, freed from all content, in his own image. This closure on the self and this second coming of the transparency of the present embody an unrecognized difference; and because of the endless self-reference of cinema and its self-sufficiency, there is an occultation of the effect of the image and the cinematic apparatus, in themselves and in their relation to each other, which seems to require breaks and intervals, a self-reflexive turning-in of cinema on itself, a sort of distancing, as it were a historicization of the raw material, absent from Vertov but discernible in Godard, although he uses this historicization to set reality at a distance and as the starting point of a new poetics.

This self-reflexive phase of cinema appeared when the consensus aesthetic sometimes called "the realisms" crumbled with the Second World War, and was inaugurated by Welles whose background in theatre and radio – in other words, words – detached him somewhat from the immediately obvious character of the image. Hence his close attention to the difference between word and image, to their relationship and to the question of the image itself, which would be seen, rather differently, in Godard. Welles was also the forerunner of the Nouvelle Vague in recognizing himself as a newcomer and placing himself in relation to a history of cinema not only by departing from Ford's classicism, which he had studied closely in order to do something different, but by intensive viewing of old movies in Hollywood and at the Museum of Modern Art in New York. This awareness of the historicity of raw material and form, which imbued Welles's work with a serious approach to United States history, also introduces a difference between the image of reality and the reality of image, whereas the omnipotent magic of Hollywood postulated their identity and unity. *Citizen Kane* and *The Lady from Shanghai* are made in reference to two opposing functions of the cinematic image, treated on one hand as a support for news, communications and media and on the other as Hollywood-fiction ice palace and mirage. If *The Lady from Shanghai* – a jarring mixture of lyricism and reflex destructiveness – had not been interfered with and cut, one could see more clearly what the early Godard owes to that deconstruction of Hollywood rhetoric, codes and imagery through distance, ironic repetition and shooting in outdoor locations instead of the studio.

Outdoor location shooting certainly has a very different importance for Rossellini, in whose work the specific relation of cinema to the present first appeared, again in a different sense from the one it had with Godard. For in Rossellini's Resistance films – whose stylistic discontinuity with Hollywood cinema is pointed out by Godard – there is despite everything a unity of character and place, of story and setting, because History (in this case meriting the uppercase H) was everyday street reality when they were being made. In Godard's early films, by contrast, there is dehiscence and hiatus between character and place, between story and setting, and more and more distancing and self-reflexivity inside the story and in the drawing of the characters, reflecting an awareness that fiction, actors and camera are all deployed in a preexisting world. An aesthetic distinction should be made between the world caught in fiction, or in the case of those Rossellini films in History, and an individual fiction situated in a much bigger world with a mutual distancing between the story and its setting. Reflexive exteriority between character and place could have been found in the films Rossellini made with Ingrid Bergman, but here too, despite Bergman's outward gaze at the world around her and the Italians' gaze on this foreigner, there is the moment of revelation, of miracle, of adhesion to reality, embodying Bazin's intuition that cinema is the revelation and epiphany of presence.

Something along the lines of an epiphany did occur, much later, in Godard's mature work, but in this case it was marked by absence and strictly an effect of form, of art, a certain "picturality" of image, a "resurrection of images," in no sense connected with an immediate revelation of reality by the camera. Because for Godard, as for the Pop painters, reality was already image, always had been, was overrun and invaded by images and cinema images. Like the Pop artists, Godard is shaped by cinematic memory and works in a period of growing domination by television.

Indeed Godard's handling of image and sound and his thinking about them came to be determined by the very existence of television, whose entire technique, in an attempt to establish equivalence between image, words and reality, consists of endlessly repeating "*ceci est une pipe, ceci est une pipe*"; but even technically, the Nouvelle Vague people owed their ability to shoot on location using small crews and handheld cameras to the invention of lightweight equipment for television; and they could choose to depart from the studio aesthetic, based on the unity of character and setting inherited from the principles of Renaissance art, because these principles had been abandoned by television.

Moreover, and this is essential, television had the same effect on cinema – at least potentially, if not yet entirely in fact – as the mass-circulation press in the birth of modern literature, or photography in the appearance of modern painting: a fading of the former magical power of cinema, a loss of aura. At the same time television has brought us a world obscured by a repulsive closed circuit of merchandise-communications-image managed by "concept-engineering" publicists: "reality" as simulacrum, as fake. Godard is an artist of the era of communications and media, one of the greatest, alongside the American Andy Warhol. But where Warhol sought to become "transparent," a two-way mirror reflecting the new image-communications-merchandise world in his painting, Godard "dismantles" its mechanisms and uses them to construct his "Artist's Impression," while holding himself aloof from it as the creator of a work of art fully aware that a real film today is born in these new conditions, recognizing its impossibility and wrestling it into existence nevertheless.

It is in this context, the new historicity of the raw material that now prevails, that the specificity of Godard can be understood, in contrast to Alain Resnais, for example, who seems not to have been affected by the existence of television and what it implies for cinema. Following this comparison a little further enables us to define more precisely the relation of the poetic to the historical in Godard's work. Because Resnais's early work contains a presence of the historical that is extremely rare in cinema. Although Resnais was close to Bazin well before Godard, unlike Rivette and Rohmer, both Resnais and Godard owe far more to Langlois, to his *cinémathèque* and what it taught them about cinema history, than to Bazin's theories. But while the early Resnais seems to have regarded himself as an inheritor of cinema history, whose role was to extend, finish, carry forward, a renovator achieving cinema's unrealized possibilities, Godard by contrast apparently saw cinema as a multitude of unknown virtualities, which could not be realized by developing the existing possibilities but through gaps, breaks, perpetual imbalance, inversions and reversals, rejection of his own achievements and appropriation of what is utterly new and different in the present moment. "The present as History," to borrow Gramsci's idea, was perhaps what Resnais meant to achieve in his early films. As for many on the political left, his defining moment had been the Spanish civil war, followed by Nazism, Hiroshima, colonial wars ... a History that had not delivered the expected meaning, that instead had instituted endless mourning, History as catalogue of setbacks, horrors and catastrophes. The turning point seems to have come at the moment when that left lost its convictions for good, when it was thought that "the war was over," the Spanish war obviously, bringing about the loss of Resnais's aesthetic convictions, his strongest source of resistance to a public that had never wanted his early films and was now going to impose its own requirements on him. Meanwhile another generation had appeared, one with different aims and no political past, out of sympathy with a "left" tainted by association with Kruschev and Budapest. Godard was part of this new generation. Uninterested in writing the present into History, whose meaning and forms seemed increasingly empty and ineffective, they saw the present as something to be lived and redeemed as charged with possibility, following – and this is essential – a "poetic" discipline from the start. For as Godard said when he had seen Malraux's *L'Espoir*, made by "the man from avenue

134

de Messine," what struck him was not so much the Spanish war as "the fraternity of metaphors." This is precisely where the specific difference of Godard lies: in the poetic force of his work, and sometimes its political weakness.

Godard is not interested in "the present as History," a changing moment to write himself into, but in a present to "act," to unveil, in a "present History," meaning traces of the past and virtualities simultaneously at work to constitute the present. So his art proceeds not from art and History, but in the first instance from ultimate experience of the present moment in its historicity, from the available materials of expression, and from the poetic ability to transform them and release their virtualities. In that, Godard resolutely fulfills the imperative to be modern, in harmony even with the existence of cinema as technical reproduction. This implies a historical awareness of the actuality of the raw material and its poetic function, which rejects all capitulation to cinematic tradition or to reality, to the simply ephemeral, unstable, labile and evanescent, and which does not signify the revelation of presence (something that, viewed through the machinery of cinema, has no meaning in a world already determined by images).

The focus is rather on current reality in what it still has of virtuality and untimeliness, identifiable only

135

by its directionality and extremes, and which only the poetic can express by creating it. This present can be found throughout Godard's work in the relation between the cinematic fiction and what lies outside it, even to the extent of explicit references to the cinematic apparatus and to current relations between the art of cinema and what determines its existence and its continuing output: essentially, and very emphatically, money...

Godard has always worked in the gap, the in-between, on the blurred and shifting frontier between fiction and document, in the space between art and life (his art, his life), between the image of reality and the reality of image. From the start, awareness of historicity has driven him to open out this gap, to make a breach in cinema and then make his own cinema in the breach, while pulling all the rest of cinema into the opening bit by bit. So that, from this awareness of historicity and its relation to cinema history, and because new video and image techniques, which Godard uses, have altered the status of cinema and "consigned it to history" as a single collection, outside time, of preserved elements available for juxtaposition, shuffling around, collage, montage, manipulation and metamorphosis (the same thing that the appearance of photography, Malraux says, did to the preexisting arts), the entire history of cinema has now been drawn poetically into this gap. So that the mystery, myth and magic of cinema emerge from the crucible in a form both operatic and reflective, lyrical and melancholy, a sort of "key" to the twentieth century as influenced and reproduced by cinema. Cinema in the century and the century in cinema where, in that interstice between fiction and document, image of reality and reality of image, historical and poetic, immeasurable horror encounters the magical and demonic "fatal beauty" of cinema ... along with their necessary redemption.

The poetic in its simplest definition is metaphor, correspondence, resemblance, assembly, meeting, connection; in the strong, Eisensteinian sense of the word, montage. To that, Godard adds collage to maintain a proper dissonance and heterogeneity: not so much an immediate or dialectical unity as the conjunction "and," a means of joining or connecting. But the conjunction "and" derives its strength, in Godard's work, from disjunctions, words disjoined at a distance; the poetic proceeds increasingly by leaps, jumps, lacunae, hiatuses, obliteration, ellipsis, the speed of discontinuous or violently compressed sequences. Godard's work consists not only of inserting conjunctions where no one else can see them, but of introducing disjunctions, breaches and gaps, by way of extension, contradiction or imbalance, in places where there is apparently a simple unity.

In this interval where the disjunctions and connections are produced there also appears their maker, the artist, his style, his humour. That is why Godard has a presence in his work utterly unlike that current celebrity figure the superstar film director. Even though the idea (elaborated by *Cahiers du cinéma* somewhat against the evidence, with one or two honorable exceptions) of the "*auteur*" film-maker as the equal and successor of great figures from the history of literature and art was the precondition for Godard's image as an Artist aspiring to be the author of a "complete *oeuvre*," a "corpus" in which future projects are combined with references to earlier works. But aside from that, the presence of the artist Godard, following the modern tradition inaugurated by the Jena romantics, is an internal necessity, to weave the poetic together with critical reflection. The attitude is one of implication in the very process of the work, as the latter loses immediate, objective pregnancy and comes to exist only as a collection of questions. But when disjunctions and conjunctions seem to become the fundamental order, the resulting form may even require the auteur's name to be obliterated.

A passage of this sort did occur, following a number of metamorphoses. While initially there was a shift from the magic of cinema to the exposure of that magic in its relation to the outside world, little by little the outside world, as historical pressure built up in the years leading to 1968, ended by invading fiction and determining it as historicity. The relations between the poetic and the historical in modern art having already been covered in detail, there is no need to explain again why, when a time of historical urgency seems to have charged existence itself with utopian virtuality, the gap between art and life narrows and art loses its proper role as the utopia of the as-yet-unrealized. Such, though, was the requirement answered by Godard's militant films. But the reason why these films remain watchable – aside from their documentary value on the frightening political vacuousness of people who blather Maoist slogans like old women gabbling Hail Marys in an Italian village church – is that, despite all that, there remains an element of playfulness, amplified by Godard's poetry and his exploration of different forms of expression.

Although art may lose so much of its autonomy and poetic "unreality," when utopianism takes over the unfolding present of history, that the very existence of specific artistic activity comes to be seen as something alienating that ought to be eliminated, once the utopian hopes have faded art recovers – more fully than ever for Godard – its autonomy and proper function, as laid down by modern art after the failure of 1848. What has gradually been recreated is no longer the "deconstruction" of the early days, but a construction on the basis of a fragmented world and its breaks, in a polyphony of dissonances, a very big style with a touch of the operatic, blending the necessary elements of reflection and criticism into the metamorphosis and redemption of historicity through music and landscape. Fully aware that at a time when utopian virtualities are giving way increasingly to horror, when adman's image-information-merchandise lays claim to creative virtues, to turn away at such a moment from the absolute of art, "beauty as promise," would be, as Adorno said, to form an alliance with barbarism. Believing in art "despite everything," its deficiencies and its own impossibility, is not withdrawal from historicity but, on the contrary, seeking exposure to it, going through its horror but without succumbing to it, and completing the work by confronting its own impossibility to keep faith with the need for the as-yet-unrealized. Thus does the "Necessary Angel" of the poetic arrive to save the "Angel of History" from dying of melancholy in a suffocating world of ruins. Marx, Lacan said, became the last of our Gospels by putting God in History. Although usually unbelievers, modern artists have put God into the "poetic," into the very form of artistic expression, a sort of negative mystique for a Godless era. As utopia retreated, art and this mystique reappeared in Godard's work to trace and outline the relations of redemption between the historical – charged with suffering and despair – and the poetic.

An artist certainly has to have a particular way of relating to the world through sensibility, imagination, feeling, and above all the desire for expression. But a person only becomes an artist by developing the senses and the sensibility appropriate to the materials, by becoming incapable of relating to the world in any other way. Thus one can say of Rembrandt and Cézanne that they are just painting, and of Godard that he is just cinema. This, despite appearances, is something that can be said of very few *cinéastes*, perhaps because the conditions of cinema production, based on separation of the artist from his material, hampers the osmosis Godard has sought, of being in cinema as a painter in his studio is in painting. So that he is steeped in cinema, clouded by it, and by the new image and sound technologies he has used to look back into cinema's past, by all the poetic possibilities of their historicity; and driven, always and above all, to think about the material, about the possibilities for invention, experimentation, incompletion, in a sort of permanent reflection that also includes a poetic naivety in attempting the not-yet-possible or the too-different, which keep his work open through its constant metamorphoses.

141

# *Notes*

1. Charles Baudelaire, *Oeuvres complètes*, La Pléiade, Gallimard, Paris, 1954, pp. 883 and 892.
2. On Courbet and Manet, see *Courbet, le portrait de l'artiste dans son atelier*, l'Échoppe, Paris, 1998 and *Aux origines de l'art moderne, le Manet de Bataille*, La Différence, Paris, 1988.
3. On the effects of 1848 on modern art, see Jean-Paul Sartre, *L'Idiot de la Famille*, III, Gallimard, Paris, 1972; Paul Bénichou, *L'École du désanchantement*, Gallimard, Paris, 1996; Dolf Oehler, *Le Spleen contre l'oubli*, Payot, Paris, 1996.
4. Walter Benjamin, "Le Narrateur," in *Poésie et Révolution*, Denoël, Paris, 1971.
5. Walter Benjamin, "L'Oeuvre d'art à l'ère de sa reproductibilité technique," *ibid.*
6. On the replacement of the former eloquence by silence, see Georges Bataille, *Manet*, Skira, Geneva, 1951.
7. Baudelaire, *op. cit.*, pp. 883–4.
8. See Walter Benjamin, *Le Concept de critique esthétique dans le romantisme allemand*, Flammarion, Paris, 1986, and Philippe Lacoue-Labarthe/Jean-Luc Nancy, *L'Absolu littéraire*, Seuil, Paris, 1978.
9. See Walter Benjamin, "Thèses sur la philosophie de l'histoire," *Poésie et Révolution, op. cit.*, p. 279.

10. *Ibid.*, p. 282.
11. Wallace Stevens, *L'Ange nécessaire*, Circé, Saulxures, 1997.
12. Edgar Morin, *Le cinéma ou l'homme imaginaire*, Minuit, Paris, 1956.
13. On this passage from opera to cinema, see my *Opéra et théâtre dans le cinéma d'aujoud'hui*, La Différence, Paris, 1995, and "Cinéma et opéra," *Trafic* no. 23, Paris, 1997.